STANDING
on the
SOLID ROCK

STANDING
on the
SOLID ROCK

*When Life turns out
Differently than Expected*

DONNIE THIGPEN

XULON PRESS

Xulon Press
2301 Lucien Way #415
Maitland, FL 32751
407.339.4217
www.xulonpress.com

DEDICATION

This book is dedicated to the love of my life, my best friend, supporter, encourager, lover and wife of 50 years. Cheryl has endured what life has placed upon her with the utmost grace, trusting in a power far greater than either you or I for her strength. If God were looking for an example of a Godly mother and a Godly wife, Cheryl could have been His choice. I thank God daily that He chose her for me and blessed my life abundantly because of the gift of Cheryl.

To get in touch with the author you can email him at donniethigpen@msn.com

TABLE OF CONTENTS

INTRODUCTION

I BEGAN THE adventure of writing this book because I believe our story could be beneficial to husbands dealing with the duties of caregiving and loving your spouse well. It could also encourage those who are living with an incurable disease* and having to live under the care of another.

I am just a regular man seeking to live an authentic life with a big story to tell. I know without a shadow of a doubt that God has influenced me in many ways throughout the 7 decades of my life. I lean on Him daily for comfort, advice and strength. He is my salvation. He has bestowed upon me His mercy and grace daily. I cannot do the things required of me as a husband, father and caregiver without His strength.

I was excited and concerned and placed the outcome in God's hand as I began to write. If in any way these words could influence just one husband to stay the course, to persevere, to not turn and run, it is worth all the time and hours involved. Our story is not about Cheryl and it is not about me. It is about what God has done in our marriage as we placed Him first and foremost. It is for His honor and glory.

You will see things that have caused me to stay the course and to persevere. I have tried to highlight each one as we go along. Every marriage is different so I cannot tell you what will work in your situation but I can tell you what has worked in our life.

I devoted one year to this endeavor. I prayed God's blessing upon the writer and the reader with excitement, hope and most of all prayer. You'll see times of joy, happiness, laughter, sadness, tears and all the other emotions of life. But throughout it all some things have remained constant; my love for Jesus, my love for my wife and my determination to do the right things even at times when life throws you a curve ball.

I must mention my sons: Jamie, Billy and Andy. What a blessing they have been in my life. You'll see in the story details about raising them as well as loving and seeing them grow into fine Christian men.

My story begins as a young lad in a small South Georgia town. Our stopping point will be a man celebrating 71 years of life and 50 years of marriage. As we start I thought it wise to give a timeline of my life and how the events in the book unfold.

1) (Birth-2 years old) This was the old home place back in the cotton fields of Wrens, GA. My brother, Dan, would lose his life here.

2) (2-5 years old) We moved about 10 miles away to Stapleton, GA. This is a very small town of about 100 people. I remember very little about this time in my life.

3) (5-11 years old) We moved back to Wrens, GA. We lived in two different rented houses. This is where the book begins and also where I picked cotton as a child.

4) (11-12 years old) We moved to Augusta, GA. We lived in a passenger train car that had been converted into a house.

5) (12-15 years old) We lived in Louisville, GA. Later in the book you will hear about Grandmother living with us there.

6) (15-16 years old) We moved to Zebulon, GA. This was where my father passed away.

7) (16 years old – 50 years old) Life in Suwanee, GA area. I will come to know Jesus and meet Cheryl. From there the story continues to present day.

*The incurable disease we live with is Multiple Sclerosis (MS). It is an unpredictable disease of the central nervous system that disrupts the flow of information within the brain, and between the brain and body. MS symptoms are variable and unpredictable. No two people have exactly the same symptoms, and each person's symptoms can change or fluctuate over time.

Chapter 1

EARLY YEARS

HAVE YOU EVER been in total darkness, not knowing where you are or where you are headed? I am 6 years old. Two of my older brothers ask me if I wanted to ride in the wagon. We have all had one or seen one, the little red wagon. Their stipulation was a little different. I had to get in a cardboard box that was in the wagon. I said "why not?" so I jumped in the box. My brothers closed the lid and taped it shut. I am in total darkness and can't see an inch in front of my nose. The wagon begins to move. I can hear my brothers talking and laughing. After a while, maybe 15 minutes, the wagon stops. I can no longer hear my brothers. I wait and wait, what am I to do? I hear other people talking. Finally, I decide to open the lid. I slowly raise my head out of the box. My brothers are nowhere to be found. I am sitting in an area of our small town that has a bad reputation. My Mother or Dad didn't allow us to go there alone. I spot my brothers at the corner of a building and they are laughing like crazy. The reason I tell this story is I could have lived the rest of my life in total darkness; not knowing where I was headed. I could have been headed for death and destruction. But something changed in my life when I was 19 years old. We will talk about that later on in this writing.

I come from a large family. There were 9 of us; 7 boys and 2 girls. We grew up in rural South Georgia. We had very little. I guess you could say we were poor, but so were many people in the area. We had most of the necessities of life: food, clothing and housing. Going out to eat, going to the movies or going on vacation were few and far between. Most of the time if we traveled it would be to an aunt or uncle's house. In those days about once or twice a year the family would gather for what we called a family reunion. Sometimes some of the adult men would barbecue a pig the night before. Those were fun times for us kids. We always rented the houses we lived in. Most of them did not have inside bathrooms. There would be an outhouse nearby. One of the houses in Wrens, Georgia had an outdoor shower stall. We used it if the weather was warm enough. Even though we rented, mother always kept the house clean and organized. She insisted that we bathe and wear clean clothes. Mother would always say that cleanliness was next to Godliness.

Birthplace of the Author

These next paragraphs tell how we went from nine brothers and sisters to only three of us alive today.

I lost my second oldest brother, Maxie, when he was an infant. My two other brothers, Jimmy and Leamon, died later in life after a battle with that dreaded C word (cancer). Here is a story as told by my mother years ago. As a baby, I am sitting in my high chair early one morning. We live in a small rented house out in the middle of the cotton fields. The house is about 150 feet off the road. This is a rural road in South Georgia, not a lot of traffic. Mother has fixed a sack lunch for two of my brothers as they head off to school. They walk down to the road to wait on the bus. Dan is 7 years old and Elvin is 9 years old. Dan sets his lunch on the mailbox. There is a big truck coming down the road. It blows Dan's lunch out into the road and as Dan reached out to get it, a car directly in back of the truck hits Dan. He is killed instantly. Mothers are not supposed to lose their children. That's all I will share about that because it hurts too bad.

Years later Cheryl and I are married. Ronnie, a brother 2 years younger than me, is working in Ocala, Florida. He had received word to report to Atlanta for selective service testing. For those of you not familiar, this is during the military draft. He leaves Ocala late one night and about halfway home he has an accident. We don't know if he fell asleep or was speeding. The results were the same. He hits a concrete bridge column and is killed instantly. He is 18 years old. I think that's all I will say about that, too.

Cheryl and I love to go on cruises. A few years ago, we were on a 5-day cruise. As is my normal routine I turn off my phone when we board. The morning we arrived back in port, I powered my phone up and it lit up with messages. Linda, my sister 2 years older than I, had died of a massive heart attack. I have one older brother and one younger sister living today.

I cannot explain or understand tragedy in our lives. This earthly life is so fragile and only lasts for a short time. I do know that God is in charge. I can rest in the assurance that by faith in Jesus Christ, I will see my family members again.

There are many things in life that shape or influence us, like that ride in the cardboard box. To this day I still don't like caves or total darkness.

At age 11, the cotton fields of South Georgia influenced me. I would work all day long picking cotton. I could never manage to pick 100 lbs. My old maid aunt Mae could always pick 200 lbs. each day. Yes, I said picking cotton. That was how we bought our school clothes in early fall. (Memories, memories so many memories). I still remember one of the worst whippings I ever received from my father. They were few and far between. I had picked cotton all day. Before it was weighed, I decided to add a few rocks to the bag to maybe increase the weight. BIG, BIG MISTAKE! BAD, BAD WHIPPING! LEARNING POINTS: BE HONEST AND TRUST WORTHLY – DON'T BE LAZY. These are influences in my life that I have carried with me all these years.

We would leave Wrens, GA and go to Augusta, GA. Seems like we were moving every year or so, maybe when the rent was due. There were not a lot of fond memories of living in Augusta. My dad was drinking very heavily. He would be gone for long lengths of time. I don't think we ever went without food but we got really close at times. If it hadn't been for my older brothers and friends and neighbors, we would have had a very difficult time. Someone had given us a baby Easter chick. It had grown into an adult chicken and lived outside in a small fenced area. One Sunday morning my mother's brother and his family show up unannounced. They had no idea that dad was away from home or the situation we were in. Mother began to think, what will I feed them? This was the last day for our Easter chicken. Sunday dinner consisted of a few cans of vegetables, biscuits and our Easter chicken fried to a golden brown. I cannot recall if I ate a piece of it or not.

It was amazing how mother could take a very few items and keep her children fed. Biscuits and gravy were common and if we were lucky a can of salmon made into patties and fried. By the way all of her cooking was done on the wood stove. Ironically, many years later, the last meal she would serve me would be fried salmon patties.

I can recall times when the gentleman that we rented from would take my brother and me to the store. He would buy shoes and clothing for us. He was really a fine gentleman. I think those years influenced how I would live life later on as an adult. I would have a strong desire to look after my family. After a short stay in Augusta the family moved to Louisville, GA.

I have got to tell the story of Grandfather and Grandmother, my mother's parents. As I write, I can see them so plainly as if they were still here. They were so different. Grandfather was tall and slender. He was a custodian for many years at the local school. He was also a very good woodworker. He could build tables and chairs using only hand tools. He had a large box on the back porch. It was filled with all kinds of woodworking tools. He was a quiet and kind man. I don't believe I ever heard him cuss or raise his voice. He lived a long and simple life. One afternoon as he was raking leaves in the back yard, he fell over dead and went to be with Jesus.

After Grandfather's passing Grandmother moved in with us. We had moved into a large rented house on Mulberry Street in Louisville, GA. This house had three different sections. My brother and his wife had a small apartment. Grandmother had a three-room apartment and we had the largest section. It was an older house with a front porch facing the street. The backyard was very large. I believe we had seven pecan trees in the backyard. Once a year we could gather and sell many pounds of pecans. Grandmother would also use them in the fruitcakes that she made each year. Grandmother was a short lady and a wide lady. Can you see her? Oh, but she was beautiful. She was part Cherokee Indian, so she had a beautiful dark complexion. She wore her gray hair in a ball during the day but at night she would take it down. Her hair would fall down below her waist and was so pretty. I remember every night (yes, every night) before going to bed she would read from the Bible. After reading she always prayed. It was as if she was talking to someone sitting next to her. She knew God was hearing her words. Grandmother left a lasting impression on my life. Later on, in life, I realized the God she was talking to was also my God. She lived a long life and later went to be with Grandfather.

There were many fond memories of living in Louisville, GA. In the summertime, we would leave on our bikes in the early morning and sometimes be gone all day long. There was one of those old-fashioned drugstores. It had a soda fountain or snack bar where we would spend hours reading the magazines until the owners ran us out. We knew everyone that lived around us. We had so many friends. It was a safe place to live. I don't recall ever locking the doors at night. Other than the love that we shared for each other, we really had no valuables that others might want. It was really a great place to grow up.

I guess you might ask what would be my desire in writing about my life? My answer would be the following. The main purpose of this writing is to tell the story of a man and his wife living, loving and enduring when a crisis hits the marriage. How a husband is to love his wife as Jesus loves us unconditionally. To truly understand who I am and how I can be a devoted husband and caregiver to my wife, it is important to see where I came from. God was molding and making me long before I realized what He was doing. He has a plan in all of our lives if only we will submit to His will. Let us continue on the journey.

My Mother and Father

Mother had a lot of Grandmother built into her. She was a believer in Jesus although church was not one of our normal routines. She was a devoted wife and mother. She loved her children deeply. Oh, how she could cook, even on an old wood stove. I often at times questioned why she stayed with my father, another story for another time. I guess mother would have asked, "Where would I go? Who would I turn to? What would be the best for my children?"

I am not sure if my Father was a believer. Throughout his life he struggled with alcohol. When he drank it would be for long periods of time. Sometimes he would be gone for weeks at a time. Needless to say, the family unit suffered the consequences. All those wasted years and all the pain that the family endured. The final 2 years of his life he was alcohol free. He had joined Alcoholics Anonymous and received his two-year pin. What a different father, husband and man he was.

Chapter 2

TEENAGE YEARS

MY FATHER IS doing great. He hasn't had a drink of alcohol in almost a year. Dad is quite the craftsman with steel. He can weld and cut it into almost any shape. He has gotten a very good job. The company builds and installs sawmill equipment, massive saws, wood chippers and other equipment. Dad goes out in the field every so often to install these saw mills. He is installing a mill in Pike County, GA. Dad has been traveling to Pike County for about 5-6 weeks, coming home on weekends. He tells mother, my younger brother and sister and I how nice the small town of Zebulun is and how good the owner of the mill is to work for. A few weeks later, Dad comes home one weekend and tells the family we are moving to Pike County (without much discussion). The owner of the mill has offered Dad a job running the new mill and overseeing the logging operation. He also has a house that we can move into as part of Dad's salary. Dad describes the house to us. It is a large 2-story house with a big front porch, large yard, many large shade trees and several out buildings. In our minds we picture a mansion (Gone with the wind - Tara).

Early fall we make the move from a place we had always called home to Pike county. All of our belongings are packed in a U-Haul truck and on Saturday morning we leave for Zebulun. After about 2 and a half hours, we pull into the driveway of our new home (surprise---surprise). Can you picture one of those haunted houses in a horror movie? Our new home had not been lived in for years. The paint was peeling, windows were missing on the second floor and to be honest the house was in total disarray. Mother's spirits fell, but we moved in and in a few weeks, she had the downstairs livable. We closed off the upstairs and never used it.

My brother, sister and I begin to get adjusted to our new environment. There was a lot of family time. Our daily routine was school and homework, dinner (supper to our family), a little TV time and off to bed. We lived in Zebulun for almost a year. There aren't a lot of memories from that time period. I remember a few.

I played 9th-grade basketball. During practice one day, as I went for a layup shot, I ran into the concrete wall and broke my left wrist. I am left-handed so I learned to write with my right hand for a few weeks.

I said earlier that my Dad's whippings were few and far between. I remember the one and only one I received in Zebulun. I dropped Dad off at the mill one Saturday morning and took his car driving around town. He had given me instructions to be back to pick him up at 11:30. Big mistake, about 12:30, a logging truck pulls into the driveway at home and Dad gets out. He does not say a word. I know what's coming and it did. I often wonder at times if that had something to do with me always wanting to be early for everything to this very day.

A few months later on a Saturday, we were having a good day. Mother had prepared a big country breakfast that morning. Afterwards, Dad and I took Mother's car to the service station for an oil change. This was the first new car that I ever recall our family having. Ironically, Dad had gotten insurance on the car. If anything happened to him it would be paid off. In the afternoon Ronnie and I had a few chores cleaning the front yard.

(Suppertime) There was a small grocery store that sold hotdogs on Friday and Saturday for like 10 cents each. I believe Mother and my younger sister, Glenda, came home from the store with a box full of hotdogs. What a meal: hotdogs, chips, bottle cokes and oh yes, Mother's chocolate cake.

It was one of our favorite days for television; professional wrestling for two full hours. We knew all of the wrestlers by name; the good guys and the bad guys. Shortly after wrestling it was bedtime. Ronnie and I had a small bedroom next to mother and dad. We never closed our doors. Sometime during the night, I hear mother going to the bathroom. I see a reflection of dad lighting a cigarette. Probably, just guessing, they had just finished having sex. All at once mother cries out. I go into their bedroom and dad is in terrible shape. Later, we would find out he had suffered a massive stroke. He never regained consciousness and one day later we removed him from all the machines. He passed at the age of 52.

We are devastated, what are we to do? The old family custom was to have Dad's body brought home. Everyone would come to the house instead of going to a funeral home. This was mother's desire and that is what we did. Dad's casket was placed in the front room. There were many family members and friends from South Georgia who came to the house. It was customary in those days for someone to stay awake throughout the visitation. It was almost as if it was a family reunion or a family gathering. Food, drink and laughter in the kitchen and my dad in a casket in the living room. (Influences—yes). Please, no food at my home when I pass. We carried Dad's body back to Jefferson County. He is buried in the old family cemetery next to his mother and father.

The next few weeks were a foggy haze. I can't recall how many nights we stayed in the old house. My brother, Jimmy, lived in Gwinnett County, Georgia and his business was in Suwanee. It seemed like within a short time we left the old house and moved into a new house trailer on Jimmy's business property. Oh, when it rained, we were in a mud hole. But the trailer was a new home and we were near family.

I often think years later, how could a young boy from South Georgia move to Pike county and then end up in Suwanee? I am firmly convinced that our life is no coincidence. God has a plan mapped out for us. (Jeremiah 29:11) "For I know the plans I have for you, declares the Lord, plans for welfare and not for evil, to give you a future and a hope". Suwanee would be where my story really begins. I would come to know Jesus as my Lord and Savior. I would also meet my future wife and finally my life would have meaning. Stay with us, we are only beginning.

Chapter 3

HIGH SCHOOL YEARS

IT IS EARLY fall in Suwanee. The weather is beginning to cool down. We are settling in to our new home and location. I have enrolled into the 10th grade at the local high school. Our financial situation is not very good. Mother has begun to draw dad's social security. I am sure my older brothers are supplementing our income. I am working in the afternoons and on weekends for my brother to help with living expenses. We are getting by but there is not a lot left at the end of the month.

Personally, I have made a few friends that I hang out with when I have some free time. I am searching for something. I am just not sure what it is. I have begun to smoke and experiment with beer. My new friends have introduced me to the local bootlegger. It is amazing how easy it is to get a 6-pack of beer. Drive up the driveway to a window in the rear of the house, pay and you are on your way. I am doing some crazy things.

Remember the car dad had gotten mother before he passed? It was a really nice car and remember it was paid off. Mother allows me to drive it with some reluctance. There is a road near the lake with some large steep hills. Everyone calls this area "thrill-hill or tickle-hill". A couple of my friends and I go over one night. This is not the first time we have done this crazy thing. We are jumping over the hills fast enough that the car becomes airborne. Oh, at the time, it was so much fun. We are going way too fast. The car leaves the ground and when it comes down, it hits so hard that the oil pan slams the roadway. Seconds later the oil light comes on. We have torn a hole in the bottom of the pan. We pull over and oil is everywhere. What are we to do? My friend, Allen, walks over to a house and asks to use the phone. No cell phones in these days. Allen calls his dad and about 1 hour later he shows up. We pull the car to Allen's house. It is super late. We will fix the car tomorrow and Allen's dad carries me home. Needless to say, it was an unpleasant experience when I explained to mother that something weird had happened to her car. The following day, with the help of Allen's dad, we repaired mother's car. I don't remember driving for a few weeks afterwards.

Without a lot of effort, I passed the 10th grade and was promoted to the 11th grade. That summer I worked for my brother in his construction business. I am 17 years old. Summer becomes a big party. I am spending a lot of time with some of my brother's workers. My brother flies me down to Jacksonville, Florida to meet some of his workers on a job site for a few days. These guys are something else. The first night I am with them, we carry the rental car out on the beach. The next morning, we awake on the beach. The car is covered in sand inside and out. We must've lost our minds. The devil can take on many forms, even cans of beer. Am I on the road to destruction? Remember the darkness? I may not have been in total darkness but it sure was awful cloudy. I am still searching for something. I am not sure what. Summer comes and goes and I start the 11th grade. My brother's shop has closed and he is doing work only on job sites. I have no job. How I would love to play football but that is impossible. I must work.

There is a mill that makes sand bags and other items for the military in Buford, GA. It operates 24 hours a day and they are hiring for the second shift, 4pm to 12pm. Two of my friends and I put in an application and are hired immediately. This would be my home after school each day for my junior and senior years of high school. The job was not that hard but the hours were long and I got very little sleep.

I had a math teacher, Mr. Smelley, and he had no idea that I was working 40 hours a week and going to school. I could hardly hold my eyes open in his class. The schools are not air conditioned at this time. He moved me over next to the windows hoping the fresh air would keep me awake but it didn't. The next move was to the front row of the class. If I dosed off, Nathan would take the old metal trashcan and slam it on the floor next to me. Some kind of way I passed his class. Later on, in life he became my Sunday school teacher and one of my best friends. I would later speak at our church upon his retirement.

Another year comes and goes. I pass the 11th grade and am promoted to the 12th grade. It is another summer working construction. I haven't found what I am looking for. I have experimented with lots of things. Something is missing. My senior year of high school starts and I will turn 19 in November. I begin to explore the options of college and how I could possibly afford it. I think I would like to do something in the engineering field. With the help of my high school counselor, I begin to take courses required for that field of study.

I keep spotting this girl and she catches my eye every time I see her. Who is she? One of my friends tells me that her name is Cheryl and she only lives a few miles from me. There is a little difference. I live on one side of the creek in a house trailer. She lives on the other side in a large brick home. Would she even consider going on a date? Well, I wouldn't know until I ask. Early October I ask and to my amazement she said yes. Our first date was at Buford Drive-In and the movie was Thunder Road. I think I put my arm around her and maybe even a peck on the cheek. There was something very special about her. I was totally attracted to her. Little did I know this moment would last a lifetime. I begin to see her quite a bit and even began to go to church with her.

Chapter 4

MY ROAD TO JESUS

I HAD ALWAYS believed there is a God, a Creator and a Supreme Being. I didn't know this Jesus. Cheryl begins to tell me who He was and what He had done in her life and also how He could change my life. In May of 1968 at a local church in Suwanee, GA, my life would change forever. I accepted Jesus as Lord and Savior of my life. What I had been looking for was realized and my life changed from darkness to light.

Let us look at the diagram of God's design, our brokenness and the answer (Jesus).

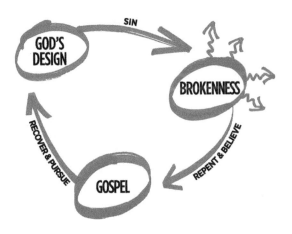

As I tell where I was in my life at this time, would you think about where you are in this stage of your life?

God has a design for you and me. We are created in His image and we are blessed by Him. But sin becomes a part of us and we go our own way. We fall into a life of brokenness. We look to money, success, being nice, church, drugs, sex, and alcohol and then on and on we could go. But nothing works; we are in total darkness (remember the red wagon!). I was deep in the middle of brokenness. I was headed for death and destruction. So, what was the answer? Turn, Repent and Believe in JESUS

Jesus came to earth and lived a sinless life, died a terrible death on the cross for you and I. Death could not hold Him (He is God). He conquered death and arose on the third day and hundreds saw Him after the resurrection. He would ascend into heaven to prepare a place for us. Jesus did all the work on the cross, once and for all. We only have to believe. Once we believe, we have a relationship with a Holy God and eternal life. When we believe, we should recover and pursue a life of light growing closer and closer to Jesus.

Now does this mean I will never sin? Absolutely not. There will be times when I sin, when I do the wrong things but Jesus has already covered my sins and yours, past, present and future with His precious blood on the cross. Does this give us a free pass to live a life of sin? Absolutely not. When we turn and believe, the Holy Spirit comes into our heart. He will convict us of sin and we should confess and repent and turn away from it.

Jesus is real in my life. Without Him, I can do nothing. He is my strength every day of my life. Maybe you are in a situation where your spouse is challenged, physically or mentally, or if there are problems within the marriage relationship. If you are doing the duties of spouse and caregiver and you don't know Jesus, I can promise you that you will surely fail. If you don't know Him, ask Jesus to come into your life. Believe in Him, it will change everything. (JESUS) Take time to look at the scriptures; God's word trumps anything I could possibly say.

Chapter 5

MEMORIES THAT LAST FOREVER

LITTLE DID I know that God would use me as a messenger to three of my brothers. After I witnessed to Ronnie, He accepted Christ two weeks later. Ronnie would be killed in a car accident one year later. Jimmy and Leamon stories are later in the book. I rest in the assurance that I will see them again.

High school is coming to a close. I have been accepted at Southern Tech. It is a 2-year college that offers an associate degree in engineering.

Cheryl and I are becoming quite close. We spend a lot of time together. I am almost a fixture at her house. Her mother and dad are really nice people but I am not sure at first if they thought very much of me or if they even wanted me to date their daughter. But as time goes on, I think they see I am ok. Later in life Cheryl's dad would become a father figure to me. He and I would share many good times working around their land and boating and fishing. I truly grew to love Harold and Dell.

Cheryl has a younger brother, Danny. He got me into a lot of trouble with Harold one time. Cheryl and I were going to the ballgame and asked Danny if he would like to go. When we get back home, Danny tells Harold that I was speeding. I wasn't but it took a while to regain Harold's trust. Years later Danny and his wife, Lisa, have become dear friends that I truly love.

Graduation is approaching. Cheryl has been accepted to Mercer University in Chamblee, Ga. We are looking forward to the summer. We should be able to spend a lot of time together before going to school. There is something happening between the two of us. Could it be love, could it be? I am so happy when I am with her. She lights up my world.

It is another summer of working construction for my brother. I am running a crew erecting metal buildings. I am 19 years old and the oldest one on my crew. They are just kids, 17 and 18. Mike is my sister- in- law's brother and only 17. We are traveling all over North Georgia erecting buildings. We stay out of town during the week quite a lot. Sometimes I drive back to Suwanee to see Cheryl.

I tell this story because we will all have crisis in our lives. I am not sure how I would have handled this situation a few months ago before I knew Jesus. It is a glorious summer morning in North Georgia. We have been in Cleveland, Ga. for about 2 weeks. We are erecting a roof system that will be used to store wood shavings for chicken houses.

The crew and I are staying in one of those local roadside motels. Basically, just a place to sleep. It is not very nice but it is very cheap. My brother and his wife are in town in a pretty nice hotel. I rise early each morning and go to the others rooms and wake them so we can get started while it is still cool. I look into one of the rooms. Somehow these 2 guys have broken down one of the beds, horse playing I suppose. Their fix, which worked quite well, was to shore up one corner of the bed with empty beer cans. I am sure my brother was charged for the damage. We all get dressed in our normal attire: tennis shoes, cut off blue jeans and a t-shirt that will come off later in the morning. If anyone saw our tan, they would think we had been on the beach all summer.

After a quick breakfast, we are off to the job site. We have all the steel up and about half the roof sheets in place. We have been on the roof no more than ten minutes. The roof sheets have some moisture from the dew on them. Everyone begins to get out the tools and electrical cords. I look back and Mike is not running but he is walking really fast, down the slope of the roof. Before I could say a word, Mike slips and falls over the edge of the building. The ground is 30 feet below. I am not sure how I got off the roof that morning. I believe I slid down one of the steel columns. I was next to Mike within seconds. He had fallen head first onto a concrete footing. I bent down and placed his head in my lap. A small amount of blood was in the corner of his mouth. Dear God what am I to do? Seconds later Mike would breathe his last breath. Someone ran next door and called for an ambulance, in the blink of an eye from life to death.

The next few days were terrible. The viewing, the funeral and the guilt of thinking maybe I could have prevented this from happening. All I could fall back on was that God was in charge and He knows all things. I do not know if Mike was a believer. I had talked to him a few times about Jesus. I pray to this very day that Jesus lived within him.

One of the hardest things I suppose I have ever done was going back and completing the project. Three members of the crew refused to go back but over the course of 2 weeks we finished the building and left Cleveland. The memories of that morning are still with me to this very day.

Chapter 6

COLLEGE, MARRIAGE & MILITARY

COLLEGE

THE SUMMER HAS come and gone. College at Southern Technical Institute has begun and I didn't realize how tough this was going to be. I guess you could say I hadn't planned very well in high school. Chemistry is giving me all kinds of problems. If only I can get though these first few quarters.

Financially, I saved enough money during the summer to get me through for a while. I will have to get a job beginning next quarter.

Cheryl has also started college at Mercer University and she is doing really well. She is very smart and shouldn't have any problems. I knew that all along.

The first quarter comes to a close. I have passed all my classes, even chemistry. I gained 21 hours the first quarter and began to register for winter quarter classes. My brother,

Leamon, works for a company that builds railcars in Chamblee, Ga. They have a plant in Decatur, GA that operates 24 hours a day. He helps me get a job on second shift from 4pm to 12pm each day. This would become my schedule for the next year. I would leave Suwanee in the early morning, travel 40 miles to Marietta for classes. I scheduled my classes to be over around 2 or 2:30. I would leave school and travel 25 miles to Decatur for work, from 4 pm to 12 pm. I moved material around and stocked work areas for production shift. I left Decatur and traveled 29 miles back home, arriving around 12:45. The next day would be the same routine. Needless to say, I lived on coffee and no-doze pills. I guess you have heard (God is my co-pilot). There were many nights that He was far more than a co-pilot. He protected me and kept me safe. I can recall one night that I ran straight thru a red light with a police sitting at the intersection. He stopped me and only gave me a warning and told me to go get some sleep. Yes, God was looking after me and He had things for me to do down the road of life. How I loved the weekends, two reasons, I could get some sleep and most important see Cheryl.

We are becoming really close. I have very deep feelings for her. Yes, I have said those words (I love you). We sometimes talk; would there possibly be any way that we could marry? How we would like to share our life together forever. During the week when I am not with her there is such an empty place within my heart. I had finished one year of school and was on track to graduate. The college has a Co-op program. You go to school full time one quarter and the next quarter you work full time. This extends the time it takes to graduate but financially this maybe my best option. Could this be our out for getting married? If Cheryl would sacrifice by working full time and going to school part time, I could work three months and go to school for three months and work part time. Difficult, but doable. We just believed we could swing this thing, knowing fully that Jesus would need to be a controlling part of this union. Now, finding the right time to tell her parents. I am not sure of their reaction. Cheryl and I have to be fully prepared and on the same page when we make the announcement.

It is early September; Cheryl and I are playing cards with her parents. It seemed like the perfect time. After about 3 times to the bathroom, I make the announcement. Well, they didn't scream or shout. They began to ask us how we could afford it and if the timing was right. After hours of talking, about midnight, I left Cheryl's house fully convinced we could do this.

Our plans were to be married in November around the Thanksgiving holidays. We would have a small church wedding and reception at Suwanee First Baptist. Our honeymoon would be in Chattanooga, Tenn. for a couple of days while we are off work. We are so in love and so excited we can hardly wait. In only a few weeks we will be man and wife. Where are we going to live? Near Southern Iron, the company that I will co-op with are some cheap apartments that would be convenient for us. We talk to the management of the apartments. We only need a one-bedroom apartment, so they agree to make a one bedroom from a two bedroom. This is the truth I kid you not. They nail a piece of plywood over the door going into the second bedroom. We have our one-bedroom apartment. The apartment next door is converted to a three-bedroom apartment. Three single girls move in next to our apartment and how they loved to party. Sleep was not possible on Friday and Saturday nights. Things are falling into place. This seems like a good time to stop and reflect on marriage and what God has to say about it.

MARRIAGE

After 50 years I believe Cheryl and I know why our marriage has endured the test of time. We have tried to use God's outline in all areas of our marriage. Have we failed at times? We surely have. But both of us realize we can't do this alone. God needs to be placed at the top of the marriage triangle. God in the very beginning (Genesis 2) said, "It is not good for man to be alone. I will make him a helper fit for him". She shall be called woman. Genesis 2: 24 "Therefore a man shall leave his father and his mother and hold fast to his wife and they shall become one flesh". This is a profound statement and cannot be taken lightly. The marriage relationship should have God placed first and foremost. Love God and love your wife as God loves us. Ephesians 5 tells us. "Husbands love your wife as Christ loved the church and gave Himself up for her." Christ died for us. "In the same way husband should love their wives as their own bodies. He who loves his wife loves himself."

The wife has responsibilities in the marriage relationship also. She should be his helper, encourager, supporter and the love of his life. Marriage cannot be taken lightly. It should be a lifelong commitment. There will be ups and downs in any relationship but always, always place Christ at the top and you and your wife under His master plan.

Back to the story, we are married on Thanksgiving afternoon and leave for Chattanooga, Tenn. for a couple of days. While we are gone, Cheryl's father and brother move our few belongings into the apartment. This is where we will live for the next year and a half. We have very little money and go to Cheryl's mother and dad's house quite often for dinner. We have each other; I guess you could say we were living on love. We begin the routine of working and going to school. It seems like one of us is in school or at work most of the time. How many of you have seen an American Motors Rambler? This is our mode of transportation. It was the ugliest car you have ever seen. Each day I would carry a gallon of water and a quart of oil with me. It always needed water or oil. After almost three years I would graduate from college. Cheryl and I had persevered and endured the hardships of young married life to see the end results. Another chapter in our life would begin very soon.

MILITARY SERVICE

It is 1971 the United States is totally involved in Viet Nam. I have been on a college deferment. Cheryl talks to a lady at the selective service office. My number for being drafted will come up in the next two months. I had rather serve in the Navy. I go down to Atlanta and enlist in the Navy thinking it would be two years active duty. Before I could get back home, the recruiter calls and tells Cheryl that the Navy has a special program that has just opened. You serve 6 months active duty and 6 years reserve duty. Would I be interested? How lucky could I be? Cheryl and I are so happy.

A few days later I receive my orders and airplane tickets. I am to report to San Diego, California for 12 weeks of boot camp and afterwards 12 weeks of class A school in Port Hueneme, California, which is 60 miles north of Los Angeles. After 6 months active duty, I would come back home for 6 years reserve duty. One weekend each month and two weeks active duty each year in the summer.

We leave the little apartment we have called home. Cheryl will move back home, and I will head to California. The tearful good- byes are said. Have you ever experienced that empty feeling of leaving a loved one for an extended period of time? I don't think I said a lot in the next 4 hours on the plane. My mind was wandering in all directions. What would

I experience, and would Cheryl be ok? Oh, I love her so much. I would not hear Cheryl's voice for 7 weeks. When I called both of us had problems talking; it was tears of joy.

The first day at recruit training is long, loud and difficult. The order of the day includes: box your civilian clothes and ship them home with a note saying you had arrived safely. Then, a haircut, a real haircut, issue of recruit uniforms that didn't fit at all and finally around midnight assignment of a bunk in the barracks with 75 other guys around you. This is surely going to be a different world. I am married and a few years older than most of the guys in my company of 150 men. The recruit trainer is a Master Chief (very high enlisted rank) from the submarine fleet. He is a really weird dude. I don't think he wants to be at recruit training. Nonetheless, he takes a liking to me and promotes me to squad leader and then to platoon leader. This will make my life a lot easier. During the next 6 months I will have very little watch duty and will be free most of the weekends.

The next 12 weeks of training were not that difficult. I was amazed at how many guys joined the Navy and didn't know how to swim. The requirement was that you had to jump off a platform with all your clothes on into the water. Then your hat, shirt and your pants had to be removed and each used as a floatation device for 5 min. each. If you didn't pass this test you were moved back one week and another week until you were successful or discharged. Needless to say, there were some who couldn't make the grade. I had a problem standing at attention. At the time I had large shoulders and a small waist and sometimes there would be a space between my chest and my arms. One trainer gave me a hard time about this to the point of making me do push-ups and a couple of times ordered me to suck my thumb. Oh well, I survived and after 12 weeks I graduated from boot camp. By the way, our real uniforms were tailored to fit perfectly and we really looked so good. We looked and acted like real sailors.

I have moved up the coast to class A school. I am so excited. My darling Cheryl is coming here for the weekend. Her dad has paid for her airline tickets. I can hardly wait. I rent a car and make reservations at a very nice hotel. I go to the local airport and we run into each other's arms. The weekend was wonderful, but Sunday came, and Cheryl would leave for home. That last kiss would carry me until we meet again. She will be in my heart now and forever more.

In those days, if you were dressed in uniform you could fly for hardly anything. There were two weekends I recall going to LAX Airport and catching a late-night flight to Atlanta. One of these times I was on a very large plane, 9 seats across. There were very few people on board. I went to the back of the plane and folded all the armrest up and went to sleep. When we arrived in Atlanta one of the flight attendants had covered me with a blanket and given me a pillow. The flight attendants were always very nice to servicemen.

It seemed like 6 months would last forever. I became so homesick at times, especially at night, when nothing was happening. Finally, I would leave California and head home. Our happy life together would begin again.

Cheryl has found a small rental house near her parents. Her dad helps install a floor furnace for heat. I install some cheap metal kitchen cabinets. The house is beginning to take shape. We are going to be so happy. Cheryl is working at Mercer University and I go back to construction work. As the months go by, we are beginning to save a little money. Our plans one day would be to buy our own home.

We think and talk a lot about maybe having a baby. Cheryl has insurance and so do I. It seems like the perfect time. We begin to do nothing that would prevent it from happening but over the months, she did not get pregnant. We begin to become concerned, is something wrong with one of us? Maybe we need to see a doctor, so Cheryl makes the appointment. She is checked and one of her tubes has some blockage, which they take care of. My turn, the doctor tells me that I will need to bring in a fresh semen sample. Do you know how difficult it is to get a sample in the restroom of a not so clean service station? But I do and everything checks normal and still nothing happens.

During this time, there is a new sub-division being built in Suwanee; small brick homes that would be perfect for us. We go and inquire about this 3 bedroom-1 ½ bath home that is about 2/3 finished. The price is $26,600 with a down payment of 5%. We have saved about $1500 and we think we can make this happen. We go thru all the legal paperwork and we are approved for the loan. After 3 years of marriage, we are finally getting our first home.

We are still concerned about Cheryl not becoming pregnant. Our doctor tells us our next step. Make an appointment and within one hour of the appointment we are to have sex. Sounds really simple, if we lived in Atlanta. But before the appointment arrived Cheryl stopped having a period. She is pregnant with Jamie and we are so happy.

God is blessing us in amazing ways. We are so in love, we have jobs, Cheryl is carrying our first-born and we are moving into our first home. We are developing the practice of regular Church attendance to worship our Holy God with other believers. We also begin the practice of regular giving to support His work. This becomes habit forming to this very day. Remember to always place Jesus first in all you do. As the years go by, we will see that He will always be with us. In good times, bad times, happy times and sad times, Jesus will never forsake us.

It is 1973 Cheryl and I have been married for 3 ½ years. I will devote the next few chapters to our life during the next 22 years. There will be many joys of raising 3 sons and of all that God blessed us with. How our love for each other and family grows and matures. In 1995, Cheryl will develop the first signs of multiple sclerosis. This will change the way we do life forever. As you will see later this is where our story really begins. Truly a love story, a story of perseverance, endurance, commitment, adaptation, and the list can go on and on but most of all (Love God and Love Each Other).

We have all heard the term "trophy wife". I suppose it has different meanings to different people. But to me, I found my trophy in Cheryl. She is smart and intelligent. She is athletic and takes care of her body. In my eyes, she is beautiful all over both inside and out. I felt this way about her when we married. I felt this way about her 25 years ago before MS. To this very day 50 years later, she is still the love of my life. Yes, she has MS but it does not control her. Things have changed in our life. But, one thing remains constant. That is the love we share for each other. I am a better person because of her. She inspires others and me every day of our life.

Chapter 7

20 YEARS OF LOVE, LIFE & BLESSINGS

IT IS SUMMER of 1973 we are so busy. We have moved into our new home. It was so nice to us and it felt like a mansion. The neighborhood has a lot of families our age. We are making many friends, having couples over or going to dinner on weekends. Oh and by the way Cheryl is pregnant (happy-happy). We are getting one room ready for the baby. We don't know if it will be a girl or boy. We will find out when it is born at Northside Hospital. We really don't care one way or the other; our prayer is that it will be healthy. Our life is really going to change in a few months.

Remember the old Rambler? We finally traded it for a new 1972 Chevy II. It is orange with a black vinyl top. Over the course of the next couple of years, I will wash and wax it a thousand times. It is so beautiful sometimes I have to pinch myself to make sure everything is real and not a dream. God is truly looking down on Cheryl and I. I would have never believed years ago as a kid that I would be in this situation 25 years later. I am so thankful; I am so blessed.

January 2020

As I sat down this morning at 5:30 to continue writing our story of amazing grace and unconditional love, I think of yesterday as I carried Cheryl to her urologist about her problem with kidney stones. There was a young couple in the waiting room. The husband was holding a two-month-old boy in his arms. They seemed to be so happy and so in love. The husband would kiss the baby on the forehead and hold it so lovingly. This brought back memories of our past when we first became parents.

March 3 1974

Over the past few days Cheryl has been experiencing some pains. The doctor says they are only false labor pains. Today she is not any better, the same thing is happening. We have gone to church and arrived back at home for a leisurely Sunday afternoon. Early that evening Cheryl's water breaks. We are ready to go have this baby. We call the doctor and he tells us we can save some money at the hospital if we wait until after midnight to check in. Sorry, that is not going to happen, so off we go to Northside. Cheryl is checked in and we are placed in the labor room.

At this time, Northside Hospital is the place to have your baby. I guess you could say they specialize in this area. Around 5 AM Monday morning Cheryl is taken into the delivery room and I am sent into a waiting area. The practice of the husband being in the delivery room is just now beginning to become a part of the experience. March 4, 1974 at 5:30 AM Monday morning we are given God's miracle. Jamie comes into the world as a healthy 8 lbs. 0 oz. bundle of joy to Cheryl and I. What a blessing to realize that this baby comes from God's union of Cheryl and I. Two days later we pack up and leave for home to begin the wonderful task of parenthood.

A few months later, I get a call from Southern Iron and Equipment. They want me to come to the Decatur plant and meet with the plant manager and the vice president of manufacturing. So I schedule a time for the appointment. Both of these men knew me. I had worked in co-op for the company and they were well aware of who I was and my qualifications. A large corporation, Evans Railcar, was purchasing southern Iron. Their offer to me was to come on board as a supervisor. I would be responsible for about 25 employees. This plant has over 250 hourly employees and 20 salaried employees. I would be placed in a position to work my way up the ladder, even all the way to the plant manager position. Little did I know this would happen over the course of a couple of years. They offered me a very good package including, salary, benefits and insurance. After Cheryl and I discussed their offer I called and accepted the job. This plant is very large. The buildings are old but very functional. It's an assembly line on railroad tracks; 7 to 8 railcars are produced out of this plant each day. Raw materials come in one end of the property and new railcars are shipped out the other end to railroad companies all over the United States. My responsibilities are to build jigs and fixtures for the upcoming order of railcars. My area and group of people are about three months ahead of the plant production. The idea is to have a smooth transition from one order to the next with minimum shop downtime. The smaller the downtime the more money the company would make. Those few weeks during changeover, the hours were long days and nights. I was good at the job; it was always a challenge. I enjoyed motivating people and seeing results from our hard work. As we will see later someone was checking on my progress and had big plans for me.

BACK AT HOME OCTOBER 1974

Cheryl is such a good mother. She really takes care of our son. We've been taking very little if any precautions to prevent another pregnancy. We thought it would be good to have two children fairly close together. Sure enough, we discovered that she is pregnant again. The doctor tells us we will have two children around 15 months apart. Really two babies to raise together. We hope and pray that they will be the best of friends.

JUNE 10, 1975

Cheryl is about 10 days overdue. She's really anxious and ready to have this child. It is early morning and she is really having some labor pains. Her mother comes over to stay with Jamie and we head to Northside Hospital. Cheryl is tearful; she is leaving Jamie for the first time in his life. We arrive at Northside and there is a massive construction project underway at the hospital. Workers in hardhats are everywhere. They place us in a temporary labor room (linen closet). Every so often a construction worker would come through the room with tools or materials. I guess it was quite a show for them and us. This time is going to be different. I will be in the delivery room when our child is born. The doctor comes in and checks Cheryl. He says it's time to go into delivery. I can go with him to a room where we can dress for the delivery. As we are dressing the doctor tells me to not leave any valuables in the room because they could get stolen. As we go into the delivery room, he tells me to stand in an area near Cheryl's head. He also says I can leave at any time if I need to.

I am standing near Cheryl's head but with a mirror on the wall I can see everything that's going on down below. All of a sudden, the doctor reaches up inside Cheryl and tells us he has turned the baby from head up to head down. With the help of forceps our baby is born. William Kevin Thigpen (Billy) is born at 1:10 in the afternoon. He is a healthy 9 lbs. 4 oz. boy. Folks without a doubt, I have just witnessed a miracle that only God could have done. In a couple of days, we bring Billy home. Jamie is so excited and calls Billy "my baby". The joys of raising two sons would begin. Cheryl will have her hands full. There were many days I left for work with them sleeping and many days I came home after they were in the bed. I believe that chasing that almighty dollar truly deprived me of many of the joys of seeing my sons grow. Men, we need to be so careful with that line between work and family. It has to be a mix of both but family has to take priority.

Shortly after Billy is born, my job is going so well. I am promoted to superintendent of half the plant. I have 125 employees with nine supervisors that are under my direction. It's a heavy load but I am ready for the task at hand. I am meeting tight schedules, motivating people both men and women. The quality of the work produced and satisfying inspectors for the railroad were all a part of my job. The hours were long but the pay was very good. I'm in the office with shirt and tie about half the time and in the plant with dirty hands the other half. My area of the plant begins to exceed all expectations from upper management.

Eight months later, I'm called to the corporate office. I am informed that my plant manager is being promoted to corporate responsibilities. The plan is for me to move to assistant plant manager for six months under his leadership and after five or six months I would assume total responsibilities of the plant. He would move to corporate responsibilities in charge of four plants. I am 28 years old. This is a huge challenge but one that I'm ready to accept. Six months later all the plant's salaried employees were called into a meeting and I was introduced as plant manager. I would stay in this position until 1981. In those six years there were many experiences, some good and some bad.

Over the course of the next few years, our plant would become the most productive plant of the organization. We were constantly building seven or eight railcars per day under budget. I was furnished a car, almost unlimited expense account and an awesome salary. It was not uncommon to receive a $15,000 bonus at the end of each year. At times I was encouraged to spend money: update equipment, remodel offices and office furniture, place in storage extra welding equipment and upgrade our buildings. I guess it was not good for one plant to outshine the other plants from a corporate standpoint.

My job as plant manager was twofold. Manage the plant to the highest level of quality and quantity on a daily basis and also see that our customers were taken care of. Seems like we always had railroad officials or inspectors in town. They would stay at some of the finest hotels in Atlanta. We would entertain them at some of the five-star restaurants on many occasions. We always had season tickets to Atlanta's baseball and basketball teams. It was not unusual to charge $1000-$1200 for an evening meal. On one occasion one of the inspectors ordered the $300 bottle of wine. When it arrived at the table, he didn't like the aroma or taste and sent it back. We were charged for that bottle and his next choice. It was not unusual for me to arrive at the plant 6:30 AM and not return home until after midnight.

DAY TO DAY EXPERIENCES OF MANAGING A MANUFACTURING PLANT

I am out in the plant one afternoon. Robert is one of our longtime employees. He drives one of our forklifts. As I walked by, he is working on something inside the motor area. The forklift is running and Robert gets his hand down near the fan blade. The blade hits his gloved hand. He pulls his hand back and slings his glove to the ground. One of his fingers is inside his glove. Robert has the highest threshold of pain I have ever seen. He grasped his hand and applied pressure to stop the bleeding. He is carried to the hospital and his finger is sewn back on. Four weeks later Robert would return to work.

Many of our employees ride the bus to work and they really dress for the occasion, suits and ties. After arriving in the locker room, they change into coveralls, which may not get washed too often. I'm in the office early one morning doing some much-needed paperwork. I hear my hallway door open. In comes Bobby. Bobby is a huge man, but is dressed in only his underwear (boxer shorts). He says, "Mr. Thigpen, that blankety-blank drill done tore my clothes completely off of me. What am I to do?" "Well, Bobby, I suppose you got to get some more coveralls; you can't work in your boxers". Bobby is sent to the equipment room and he is given a pair of disposable painter's coveralls and back to work he goes. What a way to start the day.

Friday evening, I arrived home after a very long and busy week. I'm looking forward to a weekend of rest and relaxation with Cheryl and the boys. We go out to dinner and back home. How nice to have some free time with my family. The boys are up late, playtime with dad. Around 11 PM we go to bed. At 2 AM in the morning the phone rings. Tommy, my material handling supervisor, says. "I'm leaving all the keys on your desk. I've done something very stupid." "What's happened, Tommy?" "I've overloaded the crane in building number four and it's collapsed onto the floor". "What did you say Tommy? Don't leave, I will be at the plant in one hour". When I arrive building four is a disaster. One of the 30-ton cranes is in the floor, electrical wires and cables are torn loose everywhere. Without this section of the building Monday we could lose production of eight or more railcars and thousands and thousands of dollars. "Tommy you and your people are staying; get all of them together and tell them we will go home when we finish this mess". I get on the phone and begin calling in some of my key people, both salaried and hourly. When everyone arrives at around 9 AM Saturday morning, I bring them all together and explain the scope of the work and how important it is to be operational by 7 AM Monday morning. We worked Saturday, Saturday evening, Saturday night, Sunday morning and Sunday afternoon. At 3:30 PM Sunday afternoon, we power up the crane and it is operational. After over 30 hours of nonstop work, we are ready for production on Monday morning. What an organization of employees! I am so proud of them all and will reward them accordingly. We all go home for a few hours of much-needed rest. Monday is just around the corner.

Late July, the plant is about six weeks into an order of 1200 coal cars. This has been a difficult changeover. Almost all of our jigs and fixtures were redesigned. Finally, production is beginning to settle into a routine of eight cars per day with minimum overtime. This seems like a good time for me to take a few days off.

There is a lake we love to go to near Jacksonville, Florida. Our plan was for Cheryl and the boys to ride down with her parents. I would fly down the next day. They leave Monday and I have a flight for Tuesday afternoon. I leave the plant Tuesday at about lunch and go to the airport. I will have four days with the family. I am so excited. The boys love the water and they swim like fish. When I arrive at the cottage, it is straight to the dock for an afternoon of play with Jamie and Billy.

The fish are biting really well. The next morning, Cheryl's dad and I are in the boat about 100 yards from the dock. We are catching the daylights out of the blue gills, some close to a pound. We are having so much fun; fish fry tonight. All at once I see Cheryl standing on the dock and she is waving for me to come in. What in the world does she need? When we get back to the dock, she tells me I need to call the plant. I get on the phone with Gordon, assistant plant manager. Our workforce of 250 employees has gone on strike (wildcat) because it's too hot in the plant. We need more fans they say. "Tell the union representatives I need to meet at 6 AM on Thursday morning followed by all employees at 7 AM." I catch a flight to Atlanta Wednesday evening and I am at the plant the next morning at 5:30. At both meetings we all agree it is hot. It's summertime and we are supplying all the ventilation we can in a shop environment. "Can you afford to wait till it cools off or do we need to go back to work?" Everyone agrees it is back to work. Was this a test of management when I was out of town? Maybe. Thursday afternoon I fly black to Jacksonville. At least I will have Friday and Saturday with the family.

I could go on and on with stories from these years. I guess you could truly say I was a workaholic. I was placing my job before my family. Something would change my outlook on life in the near future. Cheryl's dad would die of lung cancer at an early age. He and Della had big plans to travel and enjoy life but that never took place. I realized that I needed to stop and smell the roses along the way. I wanted to enjoy seeing my boys grow and mature, ready to be the dad they needed.

Chapter 8

OUR FAMILY IS COMPLETE

OUR BOYS ARE growing so fast. They are really the best of friends. I found time to build them a sandbox in the backyard. They spend hours and hours playing with their cars and trucks. Cheryl fights the never-ending battle of keeping sand out of the house. They have begun to play baseball that is T-ball. In just a short time, they will be on teams at the American Legion field in Buford, Georgia. How much fun will that be? As the boys are growing, Cheryl and I began to think of maybe a larger house. We spend our limited free time, riding around looking at homes for sale. Danny, Cheryl's brother, has expressed interest in our house. We ride by a house in Buford on Spring Lake Drive with a for sale sign. It is a large brick home with a full basement and the yard is beautiful, flowers and shrubs everywhere. We call and get more information and make an appointment to see the inside. The owner wants someone to assume their loan of $32,000 and give them $5000. We are so impressed with the house, a perfect place to raise our sons. We talked to the bank and they agree we can make this happen. We're getting our second home. We won't know what to do with all the space. We move in and the boys really wanted a tree house in the middle of the backyard. I build them a nice one with electricity and a large front porch. They are in hog heaven. They will spend hours and hours of playtime in the tree house.

FALL 1979

On most days, I would call home and give Cheryl a heads up on the time I expected to arrive. This particular day when I called, Jamie answered the phone. His words were "Mama has called the fire department and they are on the way". The phone was silent. I tried calling back but no one answered. I made it home in record time. Thank God I didn't wreck or kill someone. Cheryl gives me all the details. Billy has found a way to get up in a large tree (now we are talking about a big Oak tree may be 60 feet high.) He climbs up to about 40 feet. The limbs are becoming very small. He can look over the house into the front yard. I guess he decided he could not come down by himself. Jamie runs in the house and tells Cheryl. Her only choice was to call the fire department. When they arrive, they get their longest ladder and bring Billy down safely. One of the firemen asks Billy, "I bet you are really glad to be out of that tree and on the ground." Billy replies, "I want my Mama to hold me." It's just another day in the life of parenthood.

I am truly trying to spend more time with the family. I delegated some of my responsibilities to others at the plant. I was really committed to coming home at a decent hour of the day. One of my employees had a Honda Gold Wing motorcycle. On quite a few occasions, I let him have the company station wagon and I would use his motorcycle. Traffic in those days was not heavy. Interstate 85 was only two lanes in each direction. It was a really nice drive from the plant to Buford. One Friday afternoon, I decided to stop in Suwanee at my brother's house. I did something very stupid. I sat there and drank three beers, three beers too many. After about an hour, it's back on the motorcycle and I head for home. About three fourths of the way home, I'm going entirely too fast around a curve. The bike begins to walk to the edge of the road. In a second, the front tire hits the curb. I am thrown through the windshield and about 50 feet into someone's yard. It knocks my helmet off and knocks me out cold for a period of time. To this day I will never forget this. When I came to, I looked up and there was an old lady with a bonnet looking down at me. I think she may have thought I was dead. For a second, I was thinking I had died and gone to heaven, maybe she was an angel. After I figured out that I could move all my body parts, I got up without saying a word and went back to the motorcycle. The front tire and rim are bent all up. Somehow, I ride the rest of the way home. The motorcycle is put in the garage and trailered back to the repair shop. After spending $2000 to the repair the bike I return it to my friend. I would not ride a motorcycle for 12 years. I could've very easily have been killed and left Cheryl with two babies. I suppose God was not finished with me. He had plans for me that I didn't know about.

MAY 1980

A few months earlier, Cheryl had talked about having another child. I was not opposed to the idea and so we began to not use any precautions. In July she finds out she is pregnant with our third child. Our family will be complete.

Around the end of the year, I'm called to division headquarters in Chicago. The vice president asked me if I would be interested in coming to Chicago and taking responsibility of three manufacturing plants. "I'm not sure, I have really got to think about this move." Would I be willing to move my family to the Chicago area? I mentioned this to my brother. He asked if I would be interested in buying a percentage of his construction company and keeping the family in Georgia. Boy, things are moving fast and all the time Cheryl is getting bigger and bigger with our child.

The decision is made. In February, I will go to the plant for the last time. I drop off the company car and say my final goodbyes to many of my longtime friends. Cheryl picks me up and as we leave the property each of us will shed a tear. This had been a really hard call but Cheryl and I truly believe we have made the correct choice for our family.

MARCH 3, 1981

Cheryl went to the doctor yesterday and he said she could deliver at any time. Today she awakes with pains, really close together. I had to go check on a job in Alpharetta. Danny, Cheryl's brother, comes by and he volunteers to take Cheryl to Northside Hospital. I will leave Alpharetta and meet them at Northside. It is a long afternoon for Cheryl and around 8:30 she is carried into delivery. At 9:10 PM, I witness our son, Andy, being born. He's a big boy, 9 lbs. 8 oz. What a blessing! Cheryl and Andy both are in excellent shape. The night before Cheryl and Andy go home, the hospital gives us a steak dinner. It is really special. They set up a small room with candlelight and flowers on the tables. I bring a nice bottle of wine and they serve us a wonderful steak dinner with all the trimmings. I said earlier that Northside was the place to have your babies and I truly believe that.

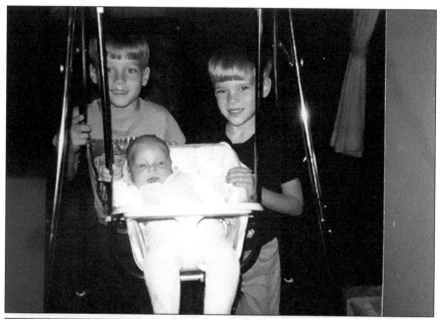

In 1981, this would be the beginning of Georgia Commercial Construction. I would operate this business for the next 20 years. With a lot of hard work and dedication Cheryl and I made this a very successful and very profitable small business. It would later be sold to Jamie and Billy. They still operate GCCI in 2020.

Chapter 9

BUILDING OUR 1ST HOUSE

WE HAVE FOUND some land in the Suwanee area on Wildwood Road. Our desire is to build a two-story colonial home with tall columns on the front porch. We would also love to have a swimming pool for the boys. We talked with our banker. He seems to think a construction loan will not be a problem. Our home in Buford is placed on the market for sale. To our amazement, our home sells in just a few weeks for our asking price. We made around $22,000 profit on that house. We move into a rental home and construction begins. We are acting as a general contractor. Many of our friends and business acquaintances are doing the subcontracting work. In only a short time the house begins to take shape.

Cheryl's dad has been diagnosed with lung cancer. He's been a lifelong smoker. He goes into the hospital for a hemorrhoid operation. The doctor sees a spot on his lung. To look at Harold, he's a picture of health. He loves the outdoors and gets plenty of exercise and always watches his weight. The decision is made; he will have an operation to remove two thirds of his lung. Cheryl is very close to her dad and she is struggling with seeing him in this condition. The news doesn't get any better. After the operation, Harold developed fluid around his lungs. He is really in bad shape. The doctor gives him the news that a kidney must be removed because of cancer. It is downhill from here. He will never be able to visit our new home. Cancer is such a vicious enemy. To see Harold, the picture of health, deteriorate to almost nothing is devastating. Harold fights the good fight but after a year he passes to be with our Lord at the age of 57. His funeral will be the first in our new church building. We'll talk later about our church and the blessings bestowed upon our family and our church.

We find out after Harold has passed that he put away the money that we had borrowed for the land for our new home. Della would give that to us as a gift when we moved in. Our home was finally completed. To us it is a beautiful home. We have 4000 sq. ft. to raise our family. Oh, and by the way one year later, we get that swimming pool for the boys. We will live in this house until 1985. We are so thankful for all of God's blessings. We serve a gracious, holy, and amazing God.

Chapter 10

BEGINNING OF SHADOWBROOK CHURCH

CHERYL AND I were members at Suwanee First Baptist Church. Cheryl had been there since she was a very young teenager. I came to the church when I was 19 years old. We have hired a new pastor. He is a dynamic preacher, but he and the church leadership are on completely different pages. Over the past few months the church has turned from worship to constant disagreements. It seems the leadership has lost complete control of the situation. There are members who support the pastor and many members that oppose his philosophy on church leadership. The time has come to move in a different direction. 93 people, men, women and children, meet and began to explore the idea of chartering a new church. We began to meet at the local fire station. We would meet under the shade trees for Bible study and under the metal shed for worship. During those summer months we never had rain on Sunday morning. When the weather began to cool down, we moved to the elementary school gym. We formed a committee to begin looking for a place to build God's church. In a short time, we found 12 acres up on a hill in Suwanee. Shadowbrook Church was chartered and a pastor was called. Many of us cosigned a note to purchase the land. We began grading and construction on an 8000 sq. ft. Worship Center. Little did we know what a challenge the grading would be. The land was covered with rock. But, with the help of many individuals and companies, the grading was completed. My brother's company would do the site work and concrete work. My company would erect the metal buildings.

The members would build out the inside. One of many building committees would be formed. I believe I served on five of those committees over the next few years. This was without a doubt one of the cheapest and fastest ways to get into our first Worship Center. In just a few months we moved into the building. Jamie, our oldest son, would be the first one to be baptized in the building. God was truly with us. He was giving many of the members, including Cheryl and I, the time, wisdom and ability to support our families. Also, he over flowed our cup so we could give financially to God's work up on the hill. There were many nights we would work till 10 or 11 o'clock. Most of us were young and full of energy. It was truly amazing what God was doing up on the hill. We were growing so fast. The members were mostly young and hungry for God's word. It seemed like every few months we would be in a different building program. We were growing by leaps and bounds. The youth was an important part of the church. They are the future of any church, even today. In 2020 we are still at Shadowbrook Church. It has changed from those early years and so has Suwanee. The church on the hill is still seeking the lost and dying world for Jesus as we gather and go.

Chapter 11

BUILDING THE COUNTRY CLUB

IN APRIL OF 1985 my brother, Elvin, comes over one Saturday afternoon. Cheryl is gone shopping. He's looking around the downstairs and upstairs and outside as if he was looking for something. Out of the blue, he asked if I would be interested in selling our home. What a shock, we love living here. I began to think, we have a loan of around $50,000 on the house. I wonder what he'd say if I said $125,000? I said to him I would sell our home for $125,000 and his reply was "When can you move"? Holy smokes what in the world will Cheryl say? Elvin said I would need to be out of the house in six weeks. When Cheryl comes home, I give her the news. She is shocked, but being the loving wife that she is, Cheryl supports my decision.

Here are our plans. When Harold passed away, Danny built a home to the left of Della, his mother. She has a beautiful garden spot on the right-hand side of her house. This area is about 250 feet from her house and 600 feet off

Wildwood Road. It would be the perfect place for our new home. Cheryl and I talked with Della. She is all for the idea. She's really excited knowing she will have all six of her grandsons in her backyard.

Jamie, our oldest son, would be the one to name this home. He spoke at Cheryl's mother's funeral and said, "To all us boys and our friends this was a perfect place to live and grow up". It had everything we needed including tennis courts at grandmothers, 30 acres of woods to play in, a fishing pond, swimming pool, large home with playrooms and three cousins next door."

The Thigpens were truly blessed materialistically. God had given us everything we needed and more. Spiritually, he had given us Jesus for eternal life. All of our sons would come to know Jesus and place their faith in him for the rest of their lives.

I meet the grader that has done all the work at Shadowbrook Church. We walked the property; this is not a small project. Our plans would be to clear an area big enough for a 40 x 40 garage- pool house. '

We could pour the concrete slab and hopefully have it completed within four or five weeks. We would put a small bathroom and kitchen area in the building and move there while the house was being built. After the grader finished the garage, he could clear and grade the driveway and the area for our house.

The very next Monday grading begins and by sundown we have a flat spot to pour our foundation for the garage pool house. Everyone working on this project is either a friend or business acquaintance. Amazingly, in only five weeks the building is finished and ready for us to move in. We will heat the space with a wood stove that I had built years ago. The boys think this is so exciting, like camping for five or six months. We make some rods to hang our clothes on and some plywood boxes for other items and for the kitchen area. The rest of the building is one large open area. Needless to say, there will be no privacy.

The day comes for the move. We're moving out of our house and Elvin is moving in at the same time. It is sort of funny but it is really hectic. At the end of the day, we are finished and will spend the first night in the garage.

Construction begins on the house

The grading on the house and driveway are completed but rain comes in and we have a mud hole. The only way in and out of our property is by using Della's driveway. Our idea is to use the plans from our previous home and to enlarge the house to meet our needs. We would like a fireplace and large playroom on the first floor with a smaller playroom on the second floor. We would also have a large master bedroom and bathroom, with a fireplace in the sitting area of the master bedroom. When all was drawn into the plans, we would have 6000 sq. ft. of heated and cooled area. We call in our friend Charles. He's been building large homes for several years. He gives us some idea of the cost. With Cheryl and I acting as a general contractor and doing some of the work ourselves, we can make this happen. We will need to borrow around $50,000 again. Construction begins; it's a mad house. Workers were everywhere; house framers and brick masons and the pool is under construction.

The boys and I are the cleanup detail in the afternoons and at night. We pick up wood scraps and bricks and thousands and thousands of nails. Cheryl will meet all the different subcontractors during the day.

SIDE NOTE ON CHERYL'S JOB

She and the boys go over to the electrician's house to leave a check for supplies. He is not at home but his Pitbull is. Cheryl gets out of the car and walks to the house to leave the check. When she turns and heads back to the car, the dog bites her right on her butt. Thankfully, the boys did not get out of the car. Cheryl makes it back inside the car and begins to turn around. The dog is biting at the tires all the time. A few miles down the road one of the tires goes flat and when she gets home another tire goes flat. He had bitten through the sidewalls of two tires. Cheryl heals and is ok. We are so thankful; it could have been a whole lot worse.

The brick masons are finished with the two fireplaces and the chimneys. That was a sizable job. They are now working on a beautiful brick wall surrounding the pool area. They're going to be here for quite a while. Seems like every day I'm ordering more bricks. You get what you pay for they say.

The nights are getting cooler. In fact, some nights are downright cold. A couple of times we send the boys to their grandmother's house up on the hill to spend the night. Two reasons, because of the cold and also Cheryl and I can have some time together. Lord knows we need it after looking at our hectic schedule and busy life. We have committed ourselves to not move into the house until it is 100% complete and totally cleaned and shined. That day has come and after 5 ½ months in the garage we finally moved into our home. We will live here for the next 14 years and without a doubt some of the happiest times in our lives. Over these years our business will grow, our small church will grow and our sons will mature into young men. There are many stories I could share about raising Jamie and Billy and Andy. That would be a book in itself. In the next chapter I will touch on a few of those stories.

Chapter 12

THE JOY OF OUR SONS

OUR HOME IS the gathering place for all of the boys' friends. We always have someone over. That was our plan when we built this place. The youth at the church use our pool quite often. We're happy to have all the kids at our house. We do cookouts and barbecues and pool parties on weekends for our family and friends. It was a busy and yet a happy time.

All three of the boys are very active in youth sports. We spent many hours at ballparks and ball fields. We even became officers in the youth association. We are so looking forward to the high school years. I coached Jamie and also Andy in youth football for many years. There were many days when Cheryl would go in one direction and I would go in a different direction. Time is flying by. It seems like in the blink of an eye we would begin the high school years.

Jamie will play football, soccer and he will also wrestle in high school. In the 11th grade during a home soccer game, he tears his ACL. After many months of rehab and surgery,

Jamie comes back to play his senior year of football. He wrestles his senior year and unfortunately, he tears the same ACL again. To this day, his knee still gives him trouble.

Billy would run cross-country and also wrestle. He is really a good wrestler. Billy won a lot of matches. He went to the state tournament all four years of high school. In his senior year he would finish second in the area tournament. To this day, Billy has many longtime friends he met in wrestling.

Andy would play football and also wrestle in high school. He's a big guy; I believe he weighed 250 to 260 when he graduated. He was chosen to the all-County football team and the North Georgia All-Stars. He received a scholarship to play Division III football at Maryville College in Tennessee. He started his freshman year.

We had a tradition at the Thigpen's house on Friday nights after high school football games. In those days there were not many fast food restaurants around. So we came home. Sometimes it would be Cheryl and I and sometimes it would be a crowd of folks, boys and friends. It would be fried egg sandwiches for all regardless of whether we won or loss.

A FEW OF LIFE'S EXPERIENCES WITH OUR SONS

We have a golf cart that we use around the house. If anyone used it to go down to the fishing pond, they were not to cross the dam; it is too narrow. Jamie, on Easter weekend, goes down and the golf cart finds its way into the water upside down. He could have been hurt or even drown. When I came in from work on Monday, I get the news. With great difficulty we pull the cart out of the pond with the tractor. It is pretty much destroyed. Over the next few months Jamie will buy us another golf cart. Jamie will graduate from high school and attend the University of Georgia for one year. He will transfer to Southern Technical Institute where he will graduate with an engineering degree. Jamie is the father of two sons, Collier and Oliver.

Billy has a Pontiac Firebird in his senior year of high school. It was a pretty little car with t- tops. One afternoon I tell Billy I'm going to take his car and drive it up the road. When I get out on Wildwood Road the car is making this awful bumping noise. What in the world is wrong with this almost brand-new car? I go back home and began to look at the tires. All four have flat spots about 6 inches long on them. Billy for some reason, I guess, has locked the car down and slid the wheels enough to cause flat spots. Needless to say, he will be buying tires. Billy will become an EMT and work in Atlanta driving ambulances. He is our first son to marry. He and Lori have one daughter, Hannah. He and Jamie own Georgia Commercial Construction Incorporated.

Andy is studying party 101 at West Georgia. A couple of times we get butt calls late at night and all we hear is laughing and partying. He was living in an apartment with his buddies. On one occasion we hear about a sofa coming out of the window and it is set on fire on the sidewalk. I am not sure if we will ever know, or want to know, all those details. Andy will come to work with me and over the years he will learn the art of steel fabrication. Andy owns his own fabrication business in Gainesville, Georgia. He does some amazing projects. I suppose there's nothing he will not built from steel. He and Marcy have three beautiful daughters Gentry, Kayda and Lyza .

There are many other stories, some Cheryl and I know about and others we don't know about. But we must move on with our story. Cheryl and I are so proud of our sons. They are the joy of our life. We love them deeply and unconditionally. I guess if you were to ask what is one thing that we tried to teach them, it would be: to be honest, not to be lazy, that the ability to work is a gift from God, and also love others as Christ loves us.

Chapter 13

EARLY SIGNS OF MS

OUR COMPANY HAS been so busy. We have had projects all over North Georgia. It has really been summertime day after day of temperatures in the 90s. I am so looking forward to some time off. Panama City Beach was our vacation spot. We planned our vacation with many of our close friends. We would go as a group and stay at the same motel. Our choice was a small family-owned two-story motel that had been on the beach for many years. It did not have all the fancy things that the condominiums of today have. But it was a great place for children. You can walk out the back door and be right on the beach. I had bought a Boston Whaler fishing boat. It was perfect for the ocean. Our plans were that I would pull the boat with my truck and Cheryl and her Mother would drive Cheryl's car down. The boys could ride in either one of the vehicles.

We get to Florida and are having a great time. They are three other families with us. In the mornings, some of the guys would go fishing with me while the ladies slept in. After lunch it would be pool and beach time. To cap off the day, we all went out to eat dinner with one another at one of the local restaurants. It doesn't get much better than this.

After two or three days, Cheryl says she is having trouble with her eyes. Her vision is doubled to the point that she is having trouble seeing. We went to a med first clinic. They check her eyes but are not equipped to do much more. The decision is made to cut our vacation short and head for home. We have got to find out what's going on. There's a little problem. We have two vehicles. Cheryl can't drive, the boys are not old enough and Della is uncomfortable driving that distance. Here's our solution: I will lead with the truck and the boat and Della will drive the car and stay right behind me. It will take us a little longer to get home. After many stops along the way we arrive safely at home.

The next few weeks are filled with doctors' appointments. I suppose every test that could be run on Cheryl was used. There was an assumption made that she may have MS but nothing definite. Strangely her vision was back to normal. This would be the pattern of her life for the next 10 years. She sometimes would go six months and no problems. Then for a week or so, she could have trouble with her vision, numbness in her hands or feet, balance problems, and in general tiredness and fatigue. It seems like the symptoms were getting closer and closer together. We're living in a two-story house with all the bedrooms upstairs. There would be a time when we will have to make a decision about our home. Cheryl will finally be diagnosed with MS and begin treatments at the Shepherd Center in Atlanta. This disease was all new to us. We knew very little about the symptoms, the treatments or the long-term effects. Over the next few years, we would learn to adapt, improvise and do life a little differently.

Cheryl's cousin and her husband invited us to go to an Atlanta Braves game one night. Seems like a good idea. We will enjoy the game and time together with her cousin. Cheryl loves Lynda as if she is a sister. Lynda to this day would do anything for Cheryl. She is truly my favorite cousin. We park in the normal parking lot and walk into the stadium with no problem. When the game is over and we begin to leave, Cheryl is having all kinds of trouble walking. Finally, about halfway to the car, I put Cheryl on my back and carry her the rest of the way. Some people would come by and probably thought that she must have had too much to drink. Little did they know. I really didn't care what others were thinking. I would carry my lady to the ends of the earth. I love her so much. Men, love your wife at all times. Lesson now learned; we will always carry a manual wheelchair wherever we go.

One weekend Cheryl and I go down to Macon to visit her grandmother (Mut). She was really a sweet lady. On the way back home, Cheryl says she needs to go to the bathroom. Today has been a normal day for her. She's having a little trouble moving but maybe it's just because she's tired from the trip. I stop at a Burger King and go inside with her. I wait and wait and wait some more at the bathroom door. Finally, I crack open the door and asked if she is ok. She has gotten inside the stall and locked the door. When she gets ready to get off the toilet, she can't get up. I see the manager and asked her to stand at the bathroom door while I go in. This is not the cleanest of bathrooms but what am I to do? I get on the floor and crawl under the stall door and unlock it. I help her to her feet and we are on our way home again. Lesson learned for future reference, always find a companion or family restroom. You do what you have to do to accomplish the end result.

May I blow off some steam? We have a handicap tag on our car. We are blessed to have a van with a side door ramp. Cheryl can pull in and sit right next to me. All too often we come out to the van and find someone parked in the striped off area next to the van door. Seems like motorcycles think this is their parking area. It's the same way with companion restrooms. Many times, Cheryl and I will wait and wait at a family restroom door that is locked. All at once someone comes out that could have very easily used the regular restroom. People, please be kind and considerate and thoughtful to the handicapped. Thank God each day that you can walk without the aid of the wheelchair.

Our family loves the water, whether it is the ocean or lake. For some time we've been looking at lake property on Lake Hartwell. We find an older cottage with beautiful water. There's always 12 foot or more water at the end of the dock. We make an offer and the owners accept. We have our weekend home on the lake. This is the first of three different properties we will own on Lake Hartwell. There are many memories from those years. The boys would be pulled all over the lake for hours and hours at a time. Cheryl has always been able to ski on two skis. But as time went on it became more and more difficult, she finally gave up on skiing but she still loved to ride in the boat. As our boys grew older, MS became more prevalent in Cheryl's life. We decided it would be best to sell the lake property. We will always cherish the memories of those days.

I said earlier that as we go along there would be things in my life that would influence me, help me to endure and stay the course. The mind can play some tricks with you.

Yes, the devil is alive and well. I will be honest; at times I have a pity party. Why Cheryl, why me? Is the grass greener or better on the other side of the fence? I look at a man and his wife walking and holding hands, I am jealous. I see a couple dancing and yes, I'm jealous. I see a lady jogging and

I say why not Cheryl? I think to myself, why is life so unfair? There have to be things in your life that will correct the course and get you back on track. Here are two that I rely on.

Find the place and the time to be alone with the Lord. Go to Him in prayer, thanking Him for all the blessings of life. But more important for the gift of Jesus that saves our souls. When we had the lake property, I would make trips to check on everything. But in truth I would go down to the dock to meditate on my life and draw closer to my Lord. These days it is early in the morning, with a cup of coffee in the breakfast area all alone with Jesus. I've always been a fixer, I try to make or correct everything. But in Cheryl's case I can't fix it. All I can do is to rely on a higher power. He can fix everything. One day Cheryl and I will walk the streets of gold in heaven. What a promise!

Do you have a Christian friend, your best friend other than your spouse? If you don't, find one. Someone that you can talk with and hold nothing back, no secrets. I'm blessed to have a couple of them. My cousin, Billy, and I can talk and hold nothing back. He and I know each other's struggles and, yes, even our sin. We both know there's a holy God that we cannot do without.

My second is a young man the age of Andy, our youngest son. He is an ordained minister and works with Andy and I. Jim and I have lunch almost every day. We have discussed life, our trials, our temptations and life together with our wives. Jim's wisdom is far beyond his age. When I struggle, he helps me to correct my course. No, the grass is not greener on the other side of the fence. Men stay the course; endure, persevere and in doing so you will look more like Jesus.

Chapter 14

TOUGH DECISIONS

CHERYL IS HAVING more and more trouble with her walking and balance. Having our bedroom on the second floor is becoming a real problem. Cheryl is so strong; I probably don't know all the issues she is really having in the house. She is truly a role model for those who are touched by MS.

There comes a time in your life when tough decisions have to be made. One is the land Cheryl has called home since she was a teenager. Another is the home we have raised our sons in. It was time to downsize to a house that was more functional for Cheryl. Andy was finishing high school. We began thinking and looking at land in South Hall County. We find a lot in Summerfield Plantation in Flowery Branch, Georgia. A house builder owns the lot and is willing to sell it if we use him when we decide to build. We look at some of his work in the area and check him out with people who know him. We find him to be an excellent builder with an honest reputation. We make the deal and tell the builder that we will start construction when our home in Suwanee sells. Our home is placed on the market with a realtor that sells large homes and estates. In less than two months we get two offers on the same day. One offer is requesting us to do some minor improvements. The other offer was for the property to sell as is. We signed a contract to sell our home for $355,000 as is. A closing time is set and we meet the new owners. They are so excited about the house. The young man and his wife have two children, a boy and a girl. They are both dentists in the Buford area. The man likes cars and he is fascinated with the size of our garage- pool house. His wife is more interested in the inside of our home.

We have to find a place to rent for maybe six months. It will take us at least that long to build a house in Summerfield. I'm riding through a subdivision near Lake Lanier. There's a small house with a for sale sign in the front yard. Well, it won't hurt to stop and ask about it. I walk in and there is a man on the floor painting the baseboards. He turns out to be the builder and owner. This is a beautiful little house with very nice trim and detail you can't imagine. The owner has put his personal touch on the home. I come right out and tell him our situation. We have sold our home in Suwanee and need a place to live while we build. I tell him that we wouldn't even put a nail in the wall for pictures.

As he continued to paint, he asked a few questions about where we lived in Suwanee and how long we had lived there. All at once, he stopped painting, looked up and said he was willing to rent it for six months. He would need another week to finish the paint. We could move in about two weeks later. This was perfect. You know I just don't believe life is just a coincidence. God has His hand on our daily lives. I go home and tell Cheryl that I have found a dollhouse for us to rent for the next six months. It would turn out to be the perfect place for us.

We began the awesome task of packing for the move. I rent a storage space to store most of our furniture. I also rent a dumpster. I cannot believe everything we have accumulated over the years. I had to make decisions on what to keep and what to trash. I know that I probably trashed some things that we should have kept. I still get grief about trashing some of Cheryl's Christmas ornaments. Also, the original Millennium Falcon toy from Star Wars disappeared. Finally, the closing day comes and we leave Jamie's country club for the final time. I am sure a tear or two was shed along the way. Construction begins on the house in Summerfield. We are really downsizing. This house will be three bedrooms, two baths on one level. It will have a full basement with only one small room finished. All the interior doors will be 3-foot-wide in case Cheryl requires the use of a wheelchair later on.

The bathroom will have grab rails near the toilet and the tub area. A few months pass, the house is well underway. It is dried in and the brickwork is started. The little dollhouse is working out great for us. It could not have been any better.

WE RECEIVE SOME TRAGIC NEWS

Cheryl's brother, Danny, calls us on a Sunday afternoon. He had received some terrible news. The gentleman that had purchased our home was playing in the pool with his family. Somehow, he jumped into the shallow end of the pool and could not move anything afterwards. He was on his way to the emergency room. Monday, we received an update. The poor gentleman broke his neck and is paralyzed from the neck down. What a terrible turn of events. We don't know all the details. He and his wife lived in the home for about a year and she left. Separated or divorced, we really don't know. He would move a caregiver in for maybe a year and finally sell the home.

We don't know anything about what has happened in his life after that. This truly breaks my heart especially when I think about all the hundreds of kids that my sons taught how to swim in that pool. I remember all the wonderful times our family and our friends had around the pool area. We don't know what this life holds for any of us.

JANUARY 2000

The house in Summerfield has worked out really well. Cheryl's daily life has become easier because we are on one level. She has begun to struggle more and more with moving her legs and walking. She will not drive a car anymore. It has become too dangerous. She is beginning to use a walker in the home quite a bit. She's an amazing woman, her outlook on life is so positive. It is important that I have something planned, that she can look forward to. Some examples being short weekend trips, dinners with family and friends, watching our grandkids sporting events and most important just quality time with each other. I try to always have a positive attitude about life with and around her. I will admit I fail miserably at times. I sometimes need that adjustment of mind and spirit. It is important to be with each other but also to have times away from each other. Every 6 months or so, I enjoy a weekend fishing trip with our sons. And, also occasionally a weekend to see my grandson in Annapolis, Maryland at the Naval Academy. Those short weekends when I am only responsible for myself are a blessing. I come back home refreshed and more in love than ever.

Chapter 15

UNWISE DECISIONS & REFLECTIONS

I SUPPOSE IT'S fitting for a chapter to be devoted to some of my unwise decisions. Oh yes, I've made quite a few of them along life's road. I guess you could say I'm a car and truck nut. Really, anything that has wheels. It was not uncommon for me to have two or three cars or trucks in the garage or basement along with motorcycles and bass boats. There were a couple of times when I bought two vehicles on the same day. Cheryl never knew what she would be driving the next week. Yes, thousands of dollars were wasted on what I suppose was a bad habit. Cheryl and I also wasted quite a bit of money on trips to Las Vegas. Over the course of a 20-year period, we would go to Las Vegas every three or four months. We even won $30,000 in a slot tournament one year. Our slot host would always comp our hotel and food plus we received free tickets to shows and events. We traveled to the world finals in bull riding seven years in a row. During those years we were making a lot of money. We were also spending a lot of money in foolish ways. We were living the highest of highs. There would be a day coming when we would experience the lowest of lows. I guess you could truly say that moderation in all areas of your life is the key.

We also enjoyed buying and selling lake homes and business properties. We also bought and sold personal homes. Once, I decided that I would like to build another house like the one we lived in at Summerfield. But, I would like to build it a little larger and more accessible for Cheryl. It would have an elevator to the basement and fully accessible doors and baths. Oh, by the way, I will build it on the golf course. We never placed our home in Summerfield on the market. A gentleman we know comes by and agrees to purchase our home for our asking price. He's also agrees to let us live there until our home on the golf course is finished. We had a wonderful home, why in the world were we selling it? I guess it was just an ego trip, so we could say we lived on the golf course. I will say that in all our home sales, we always made a profit. In most cases, we made a substantial profit. We will live on the golf course for 4 ½ years. This brings us to our home of today. Our son, Billy, was building a new house. He and Lori have a beautiful home in Summerfield that is built on a concrete slab. It has a separate garage building and a large backyard.

This would be the perfect place for Cheryl and I. We make the deal with Billy and our home is placed on the market. Three weeks later, we have a contract. We will move in with Cheryl's mother for a couple of months. I hire a contractor to remodel Billy's house and make it fully accessible. All the doors are widened to 3 feet. Grab rails are placed in both bathrooms. The tub is removed and a walk-in tub is installed. I fabricate and install a lift to transfer Cheryl from her chair into the tub on days when she is not moving well. We install tile on the floor and granite countertops. We have built our dollhouse. We plan to live out the rest of our lives in this home.

Over the next few years Cheryl's MS was not getting any better. We have bought her first of many power wheelchairs. She is walking on her own very little nowadays. We also have gotten several handicap vans with a ramp. She can drive her wheelchair in and park next to the driver. Our way of life is changing but we are adapting to the situation. We still travel quite often, even on airplanes. We just do things a little different. In most cases, places where we go are very accessible. That is truly a blessing. We never gave a second thought to accessibility for many years. I've always been a fixer of any problem. If Cheryl needed something to make her life easier, I would make it or buy it for her. But I've come to realize that

I can't fix everything in life. I have to rely on a higher power. That power is my Holy God. He controls all of our life forever.

I said earlier that they are things along the way that helped me to endure. This is one of those very special things. Jamie knows a lady that is a nurse and works with physically challenged people. The time has come for me to get some help with Cheryl. We set up a time to meet Angie. There's an automatic attraction to her. She is truly a caring individual. We make an agreement; she will come daily and do all the things that will make Cheryl's life easier. You would not believe how she looks after my wife. I can't begin to name everything she does. She exercises Cheryl, carries her to water therapy classes, does her hair and on and on. When Cheryl is with Angie, I can relax and know that she is being taken care of. Angie has become a part of our family. She and Cheryl love each other as if they were mother and daughter. If you are a caregiver for your spouse, please get some help. It will make your life so much easier. Your family, your friends or professional help will give you that lift you need along the way. The responsibilities of being the caregiver can be overpowering at times, both physically and mentally. You cannot do this by yourself. First and foremost, you must rely upon God. There are also many loved ones that are anxious and willing to help. You only have to ask. There are also many private and government services that are available. Don't be too proud to call upon any of these services.

Chapter 16

SERVICE TO OTHERS

I HAVE SPOKEN of my two older brothers and their battle with cancer. I was blessed to see both of them come to know Jesus before their passing. Also, I was privileged to be with them when they passed from this world to eternal life. In the final weeks of Leamon's life, hospice care began in- home visits. These people were amazing. They had a genuine love and care for others. Something began to work inside my heart and mind. A short time later, my mother of 92 years can no longer live by herself. We find a very nice assisted living facility. She will be happy there until she is 94 years old. Her body is slowly wearing out. In the final months of her life, she had moved from assisted-living to a nursing home. We receive a phone call; mother is in route to the emergency room possibly a heart attack. The news is not good; the doctors cannot fix her problem. They recommend hospice care. She is moved to Snellville, Georgia into the hospice facility. Nothing has changed; these hospice employees and volunteers are amazing people. In a couple of days, I had the privilege to be beside mother when she went to be with Jesus.

I began to think, is there an area of hospice where I could serve as a volunteer? I meet with hospice and go through six weeks of training and all kinds of background checks. My duties would be to visit patients and their families. I would try to comfort, encourage and be with them during the final hours of life. I was placed on a team of 10 volunteers. Our responsibility was that one of us would be with the patient till they breathed their last breath. I served on this team for one and a half years. In my visits I would read, pray, feed and most of all just be with them. My service, time after time, became a blessing to me. I normally visited on Friday mornings for 3-4 hours. I was always on call anytime of the day and night. Cheryl would also go with me on occasion. She affirmed and reinforced the desire to serve others. Here are just a few examples of my visits. I would always check-in at the nurses' station. They would give me an update on the patients and suggest whom I needed to visit.

I go into the room of a small, old and fragile lady one morning. After a short visit, I always would tell the patients about the weather outside. It seemed to interest them. I carried my Bible always and would read Scripture on some occasions. This particular morning before I left, I asked if I could pray with her. Her reply was "No, I will pray for you." This lady prayed the sweetest prayer you've ever heard, thanking God for my service. What a blessing that morning.

On arrival one morning, the nurses tell me a lady in room 112 is in her final hours. She has not had a visitor since she arrived. I go into the dimly lit room. She is unconscious and does not respond to my voice. I began to pray that she had the assurance of Jesus in her life. And in those minutes, there was a presence of our Holy God in the room. I remembered my instructor during training had said never be surprised during the passing of someone. God is alive and with us. She passed shortly afterwards very peacefully.

One morning I visit a gentleman that has just had his breakfast delivered. He is a very feeble man and having difficulty eating. I volunteer to feed him. For almost 30 minutes, he would take very small bites but over the course of time he ate most of his breakfast. As I left the room, he said God bless you and be with you. He is every day of my life.

One day there are two rooms side by side. In each room is an older gentleman in their final hours on earth. Neither gentleman is responsive; their bodies are beginning to slow down. I go into the first room. The wife is standing at the bedside of her husband. She is concerned about her husband and his passing. She tells me what a good husband, father and man he is. But she doesn't know if he's a believer, if he has accepted Jesus as his Lord and Savior of his life. As I hold her hand and her husband's hand, I pray that he has a relationship with Christ and also pray for her comfort and peace in the hours to come. I tell her I will return in a little while and go next door. Here's another gentleman in his final hours of life. There's something different in this room. His wife, daughter and two grandchildren are at peace. The wife tells me that her husband is an ordained minister. They have the assurance that their husband and father have eternal life with God. Both gentlemen will pass that morning.

Over the course of a year and a half I met some of the most amazing people on earth. I witnessed all the emotions of life and my service became my blessing.

As a spouse and caregiver, we are truly serving others. We place the care and well being of someone else above ourselves. Is it difficult at times? Yes, absolutely. We can't do it alone. We have to rely on the strength of a Higher Power. And in doing this we will receive many blessings now and in the future. Ladies, love your husbands well and husbands, love your wives unconditionally. Do all you can do to serve others. Blessings will pour down on you. And in loving and serving others you will be honoring our God who loved us so much He died on the cross for you and I.

Little did I know that God was preparing me for service to my family. Later on in life, my older brother Jimmy had terminal cancer. God used me to tell Jimmy about what

Jesus had done in my life and how he could change Jimmy. I witnessed Jimmy coming to faith in Jesus and accepting his amazing gift of salvation. I was at his bedside when he passed and now lives with Jesus.

Cheryl's mother was a remarkable lady. Oh, how she loved her family. Even in her later years she was young at heart. Della would play tennis and softball with her grandsons even into her 80s. Her Christmas gift to her family for many years, was giving us a family cruise. All those memories will be with us for our lifetime. Della loved her family but first and foremost she loved God. There was never any doubt of where she was going. In her final years, she developed Alzheimer's. In the final days of her life she couldn't even recognize her children. Cheryl and I were privileged to be with her when she left to be with Jesus at the age of 91. Jamie and I had the honor of speaking at her celebration of life service. I am so thankful to her for her daughter that became my wife. Della, your life surely rubbed off on Cheryl. We will always remember you and we will look forward to seeing you again.

Chapter 17

CHERYL'S AMAZING STRENGTH

THIS CHAPTER BEGINS the story of our life in 2010 and all the struggles that Cheryl would endure. I think it is important for you to understand her life prior to MS. She is a super smart lady. Cheryl was second in our graduating class in high school. I don't think she made many grades other than A's. In the early years of our marriage, we would waterski, play tennis and both of us played softball. We spent many days on the lake and a lot of nights at the ball field. Cheryl was the perfect wife and mother. She supported me in all my work decisions and loved and cared for our sons.

We had the perfect marriage. We loved each other completely. We had three healthy sons. We were very successful in our business. We had a loving family and many close friends. When I think about my wife, I don't believe I have ever heard anyone say anything but kind words about her. She is special and has made my life rich in so many ways. I believe in the early years of our marriage; God was preparing us for life that would see many challenges. He was molding and making Cheryl and me. We could not do life alone. We needed God's help. As you will see in the following chapters, Cheryl has inner strength that can only come from above. I am so thankful that we share our life together.

Over the next few years, the very core of our marriage will be tested. Even our faith in a Holy God will be questioned. Why us, what did we do wrong? How much does Cheryl have to endure? God are you with us? Where in the world do we turn? How much more can we handle? I said all along, I couldn't do life alone. I need God's help. When I look into His word, He answers me. I do not believe it was an accident that led me to this Scripture. Isaiah 41:10 (Fear not, for I am with you! Be not dismayed, for I am your God. I will strengthen you; I will help you; I will uphold you with my righteous right hand.) There were many times that I turned to these words. It helped me to realize that God is with us and will give us strength.

Cheryl is basically the same with her MS. She is in a wheelchair all the time and stands or transfers most of the time with assistance from others. She still has a very positive attitude but at times she is overcome with emotion.

In January 2010, we came home from church one Sunday. As I transferred her to the commode, I can hardly get her pants off one leg. Her leg is swollen twice the size of the other one. I call Angie and tell her about Cheryl's leg. She tells me that it possibly could be a blood clot. It would be wise to carry Cheryl to the emergency room.

The doctor ordered an ultrasound on her leg. In an hour or so he comes into the room. The doctor tells us that Cheryl has a blood clot. It starts in her upper thigh and goes to her ankle. He explains the seriousness of this situation. If the blood clot found its way to her heart or lungs Cheryl's life could be at risk. Needless to say, she will not be going home for a few days. The doctors believe her inactivity and not walking is the reason for blood clots. She is placed on blood thinner and watched very closely for a few days.

There is a device called a trapeze filter that goes into a vein. If a blood clot in the legs breaks off the filter will stop it before it reaches the heart or lungs. The doctors recommend that Cheryl have one installed. The operation will be performed at Emory Hospital in Atlanta.

Early February, Cheryl is in pre-op at 6 AM in the morning. Two surgeons come into the room. They begin to tell us of some of the possible side effects of this procedure; and they tell us the possible complications during and after the surgery. We begin to look at each other and wonder if we were doing the right thing, almost to the point of getting up and leaving. The doctor finally says that with MS and Cheryl's inactivity it is wise to go ahead with the procedure.

With a final kiss, Cheryl is off to the operating room. The procedure takes about two hours. Finally, I'm called into the recovery room and the doctors tell us everything has gone well. Cheryl will be able to go home in a few hours. After all is said and done, we feel better that she has a safety net against possible blood clots going to the heart or lungs.

MID-FEBRUARY

Cheryl has her annual mammogram done and awaits the results. A few days later, Cheryl's doctor calls and tells her that she needs to schedule a biopsy of the right breast. They have seen something that looks suspicious. I go with Cheryl for the biopsy. The doctor will try to go through her nipple to collect a sample. This is so very painful for Cheryl. This procedure is not successful and she is scheduled for something different in two days. This time the doctor collects the sample she needs to test. The next few days are an anxious waiting time. All sorts of thoughts and emotions are going through our mind. There will be nights that we lie awake and do nothing but hold each other in our arms. We receive a call from the doctor. She is to the point and very direct. Cheryl has micro invasive ductal carcinoma. Her recommendation is a complete mastectomy and reconstruction of the right breast. If Cheryl did nothing, the doctor estimates she may have two years. It was very obvious what would be done.

Cheryl is devastated. She tells me that she will not be attractive and is concerned that I will not desire her physically. That I may want to find someone else that is more attractive. This is a time when I have to love her more than ever. I need to assure her, to hold her and tell her that love is more than skin deep. I must be really strong and comfort her during this time. I tell her that I will never leave her. I will be with her through every step of the procedure. We will share our life together until God takes us home.

MARCH 28

It is 5:30 AM. We just arrived at pre-op in Emory Hospital. We are both fearful for what the day will bring. I transfer Cheryl from her chair to the bed. The nurses give me a bag to put her clothes in. I undress Cheryl and put on that backwards made hospital gown. There are nurses and doctors everywhere. It is a busy time this early in the morning. The nurses begin prepping Cheryl for the operation. Our pastor comes by. He prays for Cheryl and the doctors and nurses that will do the operation. Cheryl is in God's hand. I will not go with her into the operating room but God will. He will also be present with me in the waiting room. After a kiss and a hug and I love you, Cheryl is off to the operating room. I will spend the next four anxious hours in the waiting room. Lynda, Cheryl's dear cousin, is with me most of the time. Finally, Cheryl's doctor comes out and meets me. She tells me that Cheryl has been moved to recovery. She is very confident that all the cancer has been removed. I will be able to see her in about one hour. Later I'm called into the recovery room. Cheryl is awake but very drowsy. She has wires and tubes going everywhere. In the late afternoon, she is moved into a private room where we will spend the night. It's been a long, long day. Around 7:30, Cheryl is resting well and I tell her I'm going to run to the store for a sandwich and a drink. A ham sandwich, chips and a tall adult beverage are what I carry back to Cheryl's room. It may have been one of the best beers of my life. Neither of us will sleep a lot but we will be going home tomorrow afternoon. Home sweet home.

APRIL 5

Something is not right. Cheryl's right breast is swollen twice the size of her left breast. We go to her doctor. She schedules a procedure on April 7. It's called a revision of reconstruction. Basically, the implant will be removed, the area will be washed and disinfected, and the implant replaced and the skin re-sutured. This will be the third visit to the operating room this year for Cheryl. Are we being punished? Are we or have we done something wrong? Cheryl and I are so tired of doctors' offices and hospitals. God please give us strength and courage to endure. The procedure is complete and we go home finally. Home sweet home.

Hopefully, this will be the last visit to Emory Hospital. Since the beginning of the year I have not accomplished much business wise. Cheryl has been far more important to me. We were both looking forward to a few days away from home to relax and reflect, but that just didn't happen. We are blessed and we have each other. God truly has given us strength to meet the challenges of life.

Mid-May

Something is very wrong. The incision on Cheryl's breast is not healing as it should. A doctor's appointment and another procedure is scheduled. Cheryl will be in the operating room for the fourth time this year. The doctors called this procedure a rework of the skin and a complex closure. The pre-op nurses are beginning to recognize us and call us by name. I'm not real sure that is a good thing.

AUGUST 1

Cheryl is not doing well. She continues to have swelling in her breast. The incision is not much better either. She has given a valiant effort. The implant is not going to work. It must be removed and she will need to wear a prosthesis. On Aug. 8, operating room visit number five. Cheryl's implant is removed. She begins a slow healing process. The physical healing and emotional healing will take time. I must be her support, her strength and show my love for her daily.

TO THE POINT

Our sexual desire for each other as husband and wife has always been part of our relationship. Even with Cheryl's MS, we still enjoy each other physically although we do have to improvise somewhat. God made man and woman different physically but he had the knowledge and wisdom to design us in a way that we could become one flesh. My desire and prayer is that we can have that intimacy until God takes us home. Guys, nothing is changed with Cheryl. Yes, physically she looks different. But beauty is far more than skin deep. She is and always will be beautiful in my eyes. Breast cancer can be a real challenge in a marriage. But it also can be something that brings a relationship into a stronger bond.

Husbands, stay the course, support your wife and love her unconditionally. Be the man that God will smile down upon. Your cup will overflow with blessings.

I can use the words of Solomon to describe my wife. (Behold, you are beautiful, my love. You are all together beautiful, my love; there is no flaw in you. You captivate my heart with one glance of your eyes.) Cancer will not and cannot destroy our love for each other. It will only make our love stronger. Our hope, our assurance, our strength is in God and nothing can defeat Him.

MID-OCTOBER

Cheryl is doing quite well. Her breast is healed and she is getting accustomed to wearing the prosthesis. Even with her bathing suit on, you cannot tell she's had breast cancer. She's a real trooper. One morning, she wakes up and has a lot of pain in her lower back. From tests that we had done years ago, we know she has some stones in her kidneys. Sitting and her inactivity contribute to kidney stones. Cheryl's urologist's works her in and after some tests he says she has a stone in her right kidney that needs to be removed. He will use a process called lithotripsy (ultrasound) to break the stone into pieces. This will be the sixth time this year that Cheryl will be put to sleep. Cheryl is prepared for the procedure and off she goes. About one hour later her doctor comes out and tells me the lithotripsy was successful. She should be able to pass the small pieces of stone. I will be able to carry her home in a few hours.

MID-NOVEMBER

It is that time of the year when we began to look forward to the holidays. Thanksgiving and Christmas have always been our favorite time of the year.

Considering everything that has happened this year, it will be especially nice. We awake one morning and Cheryl cannot urinate. She really needs to pee but something is blocking her system. It is off to the emergency room. After an ultrasound, the doctors discover a stone in her tubes coming from her kidneys. They will use a procedure called ureteroscopy stone extraction. This will be the seventh time this year that Cheryl has been to the operating room. It seems as though we have spent half our time in hospitals this year. The procedure is successful. Cheryl is able to urinate and we return home. Home sweet home.

What a year; it surely has tested our endurance, our resolve and yes our faith. When all was said and done, we paid over $30,000 in doctor and hospital bills above what our insurance paid. Over the next few years about every six months, our insurance premiums would increase. They were making it almost impossible to continue paying the premiums. Finally, we had to discontinue the insurance. Luckily, Cheryl would go on disability and I would go on Medicare. Something needs to be done about medical insurance. To this day we still struggle at times on paying our co-pay.

As I look back at that time in our life, I can question, why Cheryl? But deep down inside I know the answer. She is and always has been an example to others on how to live when life throws you a curveball. She is a perfect example of endurance, perseverance, faith, love and hope. Neither of us relies on our own strength. Our hope is in Jesus. He can do all things.

As you will see in the next chapter, we will be faced with many challenges financially. We have seen the highest of highs and now we will experience the lowest of lows. But some things remain constant in our life, which are the love for each other and family, but most of all, the love for God. He is real and never leaves us. We can depend upon Him.

Chapter 18

THE LOWEST OF LOWS

OUR LIFE IN the construction business has always been sort of like riding a roller coaster. There have been very busy times and slow times. Some jobs were really profitable and some were not. So, we would plan accordingly to balance the lows and the highs. We had always maintained a very high credit score. We never let bills run late. In fact we tried to pay weeks before they were due. We could go anywhere and purchase items on credit. Cheryl and I were building one or two buildings each year and selling or leasing them. Construction loan money was a phone call or a handshake away. A loan of a half million dollars was pretty routine. Times were good. We had CDs in a couple of banks and money in the stock market. We were making a profit on each building we sold. Our home was mortgage free. In fact we owed very little.

Things would change, it seemed like overnight. The banks began to tighten up on their loans. People were not buying or leasing real estate. Jobs were getting harder to find.

Companies were slow paying or not paying at all. Tenants in the leased properties began to leave or not pay their lease agreement. Our philosophy at the time was we would ride this out. Things will come back to normal; they always have. Just give it a little time; it is just a small downturn. It didn't. Things would get a lot worse. Cheryl and I continue to pay our bills even when others were not paying us. We had a warehouse not rented for over a year, $3700 per month and a tenant that was not paying his rent of $2500 a month. Money that was invested in the stock market was slowly disappearing. No money was coming in and thousands each month was going out. The perfect firestorm was beginning. The money we had worked so hard for and saved was disappearing at a rapid rate. It was not just us, our friends and acquaintances in the building business were losing everything they had. Sometimes we would get together and just cry on each other's shoulder. We surely had plenty of time because there were no jobs available. Who would have the coffee money today?

I will be the first to confess, I had made some very poor financial decisions. To name a few: building a home on the golf course, buying a motor home for over $200,000, too many trips to Las Vegas, poor investments and quite a few more things would cost me in this downturn. I can sit here and say, "If I only had it to do over again". But many times in life you do not get a second chance. There were many sleepless nights. Cheryl and I would lay awake thinking about where the next dollar would come from or how we would pay the mortgage on one of the properties. Many nights we fell asleep holding each other, knowing that we would stay the course and God was in control. If only we can hold out. Here are some things we did to acquire some money. We were not ready to throw in the towel.

1. We borrowed money from Cheryl's mother.

2. We sold Cheryl's 2-carat wedding ring and mortgaged our home.

3. We voluntarily surrendered the motorhome to the mortgage company.

4. We used all of our CDs in the bank to pay bills.

5. We maxed out three credit cards to their limit.

6. We took a huge loss in the stock market and pulled out the small amount of money left.

After almost a year and a half, things would not get better. Yes, they even got worse.

One building in particular, I had paid the mortgage for over a year without any rent coming in. I couldn't go any longer. I met the president of the bank that we had used for 20 years. I laid the keys to the building on his desk one morning. "I can go no farther", I explained. He turned and opened the cabinet to reveal a wall of keys. He passed my keys back across the desk. His statement was "I have more than I can handle. I surely don't need yours". This was his solution. He placed me on interest-only payments and made the first payment due in 12 months. This would give me 12 months to sell the property. In six months, I would sell the property for what I owed the bank. It was a win-win situation for the bank and me. Later I would write the bank thanking them for giving me this opportunity.

We can go no further. We have exhausted everything that we have. We've tried to do the right things, to be honest, trustworthy and pay the ones we owe. We have nothing left. Andy, my youngest son, recommends a lawyer in Buford, Georgia. He has done a lot of bankruptcies in this area. Cheryl and I meet with him. This is all new to us. In all of our married life, we have always paid our bills. He asked 1000 questions and asked for all sorts of records. His recommendation is for us to begin the procedure of filing Chapter 7 bankruptcy

After days and days of filling out forms and compiling files, we submit a very thick folder to the lawyer. He will file our case with the federal court and we will wait on the court date. I feel so ashamed, so guilty. Night after night, I wake with this situation on my mind. I've really messed up. I never intended for things to work out this way. I'm so sorry.

The day has come for us to appear before the federal judge at the federal courthouse in Gainesville, Georgia. I don't believe I've ever been in a federal courthouse. I didn't tell Cheryl, but to be honest, I was a little nervous. We go through the security check and into the courtroom. The room is completely full of people. Everyone is there for the judge to hear their petition. After about one hour the judge calls our case and Cheryl and I go before the judge. He looks at us and down at our paperwork. He asked us how we got to this point and if today was our last option. We explained how we had paid our bills when no one was paying us. We had exhausted everything we have. There's no money left. He tells our lawyer that he needs a few more documents. We are dismissed and will wait on his decision. A couple of weeks later, our lawyer calls and tells us the judges approved our case and we will receive a Chapter 7 discharge. The emotions of relief, joy and, yes, sadness and guilt all play heavy on our minds.

Bankruptcy will be a scar on our credit for many years. It will take 7 to 8 years for us to regain a decent credit score. Could I have done things differently? Yes, I confess I could've been a lot wiser. I could've even been dishonest and hid some of our money. I could have stopped paying our bills. I could've stopped borrowing and erecting buildings when the economy took a downturn. The end result is we will never get back everything we lost financially.

But today, Cheryl and I still have each other. We realize God loves us even when we make very unwise decisions. Yes, life will go on. There will be other struggles in our life but we can hold fast. God is the same now and forevermore. He is real and he is with us always.

Chapter 19

FAMILY SUPPORT

DO YOU LOVE someone? Can you say you love someone unconditionally? Do you tell someone that you love them each and every day? Do you place the well being of someone else before you? Do you love someone as if they are a part of you? For a man, or a woman, to be the caregiver for their spouse, you answer these questions each and every day of your life in your actions. You can't do it alone, though. First, we need to depend on our Lord Jesus Christ who loves us and died for us.

Second, the support of a loving family is vital. Our sons are grown men now. They truly love their mother and dad. One afternoon I come in from work. I raise the garage door and see a new truck parked in my space. I suppose we have company, I guessed. As I walked by the truck, I see a note on the front seat. (Dad, enjoy your new ride. Thanks for all that you have taught us through the years. We love you, Jamie and Billy.) I was overcome with emotion.

A few years later, the accessible van Cheryl uses has 125,000 miles on it. It is paid for so we are trying to make it last. Really, we can afford to buy a new one at this time. As I pull into the driveway one afternoon, I look inside the garage. There is a shiny, red minivan. Without Cheryl knowing, all three boys have replaced Cheryl's van with a new accessible van. They care deeply for their mother's well being. It is not about cars and trucks. It is their love for mother and dad and how they care for us.

The love of family has surely rubbed off on our grandchildren. Every time we are with them, it is a hug or a kiss and I love you. We are so very proud of them. Oliver will begin his senior year at the Naval Academy in 2020. He wants to fly jets for the Navy. I think he will really do it. I had the privilege of being with him when he was sworn in at the Academy. (GO NAVY).

Collier has a job in the engineering department of a large company. He does some amazing three-dimensional work.

Gentry is in her first year at West Georgia College. She wants to go into the nursing field.

Kayda is a junior in high school. She is a competitive cheerleader. She does some amazing routines.

Hannah is also a junior in high school. She runs track and she is our pole-vaulter. She's cleared 9 ft. 6 in. That is a new record for her high school.

Lyza is a freshman. She takes after her mother and dad. She plays volleyball in high school and is also on the traveling team. She started games in her freshman year on the varsity team.

They are all so loving, so caring and so respectful to others. They're all truly our pride and joy. We love each of them more than they will ever know. I cannot stop without mentioning Lori and Marcy. They are Billy and Andy's wives. They are the perfect daughter-in-laws. They would do anything for Cheryl and me. We love you so much girls.

PETS

Do you have a pet? They can give you so much joy and happiness. Cheryl and I have always loved animals. During Cheryl's childhood, her mother raised German Shepherds. She even donated some to the Army that were used in Vietnam. They were beautiful and intelligent dogs.

After Cheryl and I were married and the boys were born, we raised Cocker Spaniels. We had many puppies that were either sold or given away. They were always outside dogs. The inside of our house was off limits. Then, along came Sampson. Andy bought Sampson when he was six weeks old. Andy and Marcy were moving in with Della, Cheryl's mother. Marcy would look after Della in her later years. Sampson could not move with them so we adopted him. He is a beautiful English bulldog.

I'm really not sure if he realizes he's a dog. He loves people and wants to always be around us. For someone to have an English bulldog in their home, they must really love them. They take a lot of care: bathing, feeding, cleaning wrinkles and keeping their ears clean. They pass gas, they snore, they smell bad but they are amazing animals. Sampson is a big part of our family. April 2020, Sampson turned 12 years old. He has lived longer than most bulldogs live. We will enjoy him until his last days. When I'm not at home, Sampson is right next to Cheryl. He is so much company to her.

But when I walk in the door, he becomes my dog. If I take a shower, he's right outside the door. He sleeps right next to me at night on the floor. I can place my hand down on his head.

Here are a few of the interesting things that have happened in Sampson's life. One day I carry Sampson to the vet and drop him off. They put him to sleep and cleaned his teeth. The office was to call me when he was finished. I wait and wait and finally I call the vet. He came on the phone and says, "You're not going to believe this, but Sampson stopped breathing on us. We had to place a tube down his throat. He is fine now but I don't think it would be wise to put him to sleep again." Thankfully, Sampson is still with us.

Cheryl and I had dinner. We had fresh corn on the cob. It was summertime. Cheryl accidentally drops a piece of corn on the floor. It is about a half an ear of corn. Before we could pick it up, Sampson swallowed it. The vet tells us that Sam will not digest the cob. Hopefully he will pass it. Believe it or not, two years later Sampson throws the cob up. I cannot explain it. He's a special dog.

Sampson had an upset stomach. The vet gives me a plastic bag with 20 chewable pills. I go by the shop and leave Sampson in the office. The pills are left on the corner of my desk. 10 minutes later I come into the office and the plastic bag has disappeared. I look and it is lying on the floor in the corner of the room, empty of all the pills. I called the vet, "Doc., you are not going to believe this but Sampson has eaten every one of those pills." He says "I will call you right back". A few minutes later he calls and tells me to go get some hydrogen peroxide. Carry Sampson outside and give him a spoonful. A few minutes later everything in Sampson's stomach comes up including all the pills. I guess you could say, just another day in the life of an English Bulldog. If you're in a situation where your spouse is physically challenged, I highly recommend a pet. They will give you so much love and joy and happiness.

Chapter 20

WELLBEING OF
THE CARETAKER

AS A CAREGIVER for your spouse, out of love, you place their well being before yours. But it is so important that you maintain your health, physically and mentally. Take time off to be alone and refresh yourself. Get some exercise, take a walk or do some yard work. You need to stay as healthy as possible. Don't let yourself become a couch potato.

Sometimes there are things that happen in your life that are beyond your control. This is when it is so important to have family and friends. They can step in and assist with the care of your spouse.

Here's an example of a few things that happened in my life. It is a glorious summer morning. I'm going to a job site in a new work truck. I am headed south on a divided four-lane road. I see a car headed north approaching me. The lady driving the car looks into the back seat. Her car veers to the left and the front wheel hits the divider curb. The impact with the curb throws her car directly in front of my truck. I am traveling between 45 and 50 miles per hour and I T-boned her car on the passenger side. This is the amazing part of the story. As I look up a small child comes out the side window and goes over the top of my truck. I see him land in the roadway as my truck goes off the road and comes to rest in a grassy area on the side. Her car is totally destroyed and sits in the middle of the road. My God, what has just happened? Ambulances and police are there within a matter of minutes. The child in the roadway is placed in an ambulance and off they go. The lady driver is trapped in the wreckage in the middle of the road. I've been knocked silly. I have a knot on my forehead and my left knee is swollen. I'm carried to the hospital and checked out and given blood and alcohol tests. I believe the police are thinking the worst has happened to the child that was ejected.

For a few days I was a wreck. My insurance company finally calls. They have information on the lady and the child. It is amazing that there are guardian angels around us. The child that was ejected from the car only suffered a few broken bones.

The lady is more severely hurt but will recover. I was sore all over, especially my knee. I needed help for a few days looking after Cheryl. I didn't drive for a couple weeks. My sons helped me get where I needed to go. After a few weeks I received a new truck and all my medical bills were paid. God was surely with us that morning.

In 2015 I go to the doctor for my yearly physical. He checked my chest with his stethoscope. He places it on the left side of my neck. He looks at me strangely. Something does not sound right. He schedules an ultrasound two days later. After the test, the doctor calls me and tells me it would be wise for me to see a vascular surgeon. I make the appointment and he does another ultrasound. Cheryl, Angie and I are anxiously waiting for his opinion. He comes into the room and has a seat. He begins to explain that I have a blockage in my carotid artery. He tells us that the blockage is around 95%. Something needs to be done pretty fast. I am a walking time bomb. If the blockage breaks off and goes to my brain it could result in a stroke. He stays with us for almost an hour. He explains the procedure, how long the operation will take, and how long I will be in ICU and the recovery time. Here's the problem. After surgery I will not be able to lift Cheryl for seven days. I lift Cheryl every day and night. What will I do? He schedules a date for the operation. I began to plan accordingly. Angie will take me to the hospital and stay with Cheryl for two days. After I come home, Lynda, Cheryl's dear cousin, will stay with us for three or four days. I believe I have everything worked out. I must have the operation. Also, I must make sure Cheryl is looked after. I'm ready to get this over with. The night before I am scheduled to be at the hospital the next morning, we get a call from the doctor's office. There are some paperwork problems that are not complete with the insurance company. The doctor must reschedule the operation to take place two weeks later. After preparing myself mentally, emotionally and praying for God's protection and scheduling people to stay with Cheryl, we are pushed back two weeks. How discouraging is this?

Everything is rescheduled and the day comes for the operation. The procedure takes about three hours. When the doctor sees me in the recovery room, he shows me what he has removed. It is the diameter of the artery and about 1 inch long. It has a small tiny hole in the center that blood was passing through. I'm a blessed man; this could have very easily ended my life.

Angie and Lynda are so wonderful. They looked after Cheryl night and day. My job was to recover and take care of myself. After about five days I was able to move Cheryl around and my helpers went home. I was so lucky. No, I was so blessed. During a routine physical this doctor saved my life.

I am in Andy's shop fabricating a form to hold concrete. Jerry, my helper, and I have a quarter inch plate up on the sawhorses. It weighs around 75 pounds. We stand the plate up and tack weld it to the base. As I go to square the plate with the base form, the tack weld breaks. The plate falls 36 inches down and the corner of the plate strikes my boot right over my big toe. It really hurts, so I sit down on the floor and pull my boot off. My white sock was completely red. Something is bad wrong. I hobble into the office and sit down in the chair. When I pull my sock off, my big toe falls over to the side. Blood is everywhere. The plate has broken the bone and cut my toe almost in half. Jerry freaks out. I tell him to get me a roll of gauze out of the first-aid kit. I pushed my toe back over in place and tightly wrap the whole roll of gauze around my foot. The emergency room is five minutes away. Jim carries me in his truck. The hospital takes me back into one of their rooms. Andy and Cheryl are called and told where I am and what is going on. Andy heads to the hospital and he assures Cheryl that I will be fine. I will call her as soon as possible.

The doctors clean and disinfect the toe. They pushed it back into position and sutured the skin and the tissue back together. Four hours later I walk out of the emergency room with a big bandage and a boot. It is so strange how your mind thinks. The whole time in the hospital, I was thinking about how I would look after Cheryl. My toe was going to be a problem for a few days in my regular routine. But with the help of family and Angie, everything worked out fine.

Guys, in the life of a spouse- caregiver you will find times that you cannot control everything that happens. There will be times when you feel like the weight of the world rests on your shoulders. All sorts of crazy thoughts will go through your mind. Why am I doing this? Is there a better way? Should I turn and run? Why can't my life be like others? I can't do this alone. God, I need your strength. In these times, find your quiet place. Yes, it is okay to shed a tear, it is okay to pray, and it is okay to call your best friend. And most of all, it is okay to rely on God's strength and not yours. I promise you; you can get through any obstacle with God's help. Stay the course, endure and be the person that God would want you to be.

A few weeks ago, Cheryl asked me this question. If I had known 25 years ago what our life would look like today, what would I have done? My answer as a sinful human being would have been to turn and run away. But because my strength comes from above, I would have to ask, "What would Jesus do"? He tells us to love our spouse with all our soul and heart and mind. You are to love unconditionally in times of sickness or health, in times when you experience riches or poverty or until death do us part. Rely on God's strength and He will get you through any hardship.

Chapter 21

OUR TYPICAL DAY TOGETHER

I DO NOT write this to make you feel sorry for us or to pat myself on the back. I write this so that you might experience what a day is like in the life of a spouse and a caregiver. All honor and glory goes to my Lord and Savior for giving me strength and endurance to accomplish my daily routine. His amazing grace is sufficient for me. It is sufficient for Cheryl. And it is sufficient for you. He is always with us, regardless of our life situations. We only have to rely upon Him. It seems as though sometimes in life pain can bring us joy.

SATURDAY, 10PM

This is the time we normally begin to get ready for bed. I will shower and shave first. About 30 minutes later, it is time for Cheryl's bath. We are blessed to have a walk-in tub. On most days, with my assistance, Cheryl can get in the tub without the lift. If she is experiencing a bad day, I have a lift above the tub that I can transfer her from her chair to the tub. She loves to take baths instead of showers. The air jets in her tub are so soothing to her. After her bath, I dry her off and dress her in her nightgown. I don't know how many times I hear the words "I love you or thank you". She is so amazing. I have a little step about 4 inches high next to the bed. I place her feet on the steps and lift and transfer her to the bed. Each night I turn the electric blanket on about 30 minutes before bedtime. It is warm and cozy for her when she goes to bed. I always turn it off before we fall asleep. We normally watch the news. At around 11:30, we say "I love you" and fall asleep holding each other. Once or twice during the night, she will ask me to carry her to the bathroom or turn her over. Not always, but sometimes it's difficult for us to fall back asleep. The clock is set for 5:30 AM. This is my quiet time. I read, pray and prepare my Bible study lessons. Sometimes it's just a time of reflection thanking God for his love and amazing grace.

Around 7 AM I place a machine in the bed that moves Cheryl's feet and legs. I also exercise her arms and legs. This all takes about 15 minutes. Cheryl and Angie normally pick out what Cheryl will wear each day of the week. I get Cheryl out of bed and into the bathroom. It is time to dress her and get her ready for church. She wears compression socks and, boy, are they hard to get on. But it does prevent her legs from swelling.

It is time to fix her hair. I've gotten really good at fixing her hair. Over the past few years, Cheryl has begun to have more trouble with her hands and arms. She cannot fix her hair or cut her food. Most of the time she eats with a spoon. I always try to stay a step ahead of her so she doesn't struggle with her plate. It is impossible for her to put her earrings or jewelry on. That is part of my job in the morning. She's almost ready to go. It is my turn, which doesn't take very long. Cheryl really watches what she eats. Most of the time for breakfast, it is an apple or grapes. It is off to Bible Study and church. After church, we stop for lunch somewhere or come home for a sandwich. Cheryl will get comfortable in her recliner with a book. She loves to read and sometimes reads one or two books a week. Sunday afternoon is my time in the kitchen. I enjoy cooking and I might have a couple of meals going at the same time. This is also our time together. We may discuss our Bible Study lesson or the sermon at the church. We also look at our schedule for the next week. It has doctors' appointments, meetings, grandchildren's sporting events and etc. Sometimes it's just a time to talk about life in general. We are man and wife but we are also the best of friends. After dinner and a few hours of TV, it is bath and bedtime. God has given us another day together. Angie will come in tomorrow morning and take Cheryl to the pool for her water exercises. I will go to Andy's shop for a few hours of work.

Forrest Gump in his movie said "Life is like a box of chocolates; you never know what you're going to get." This is so true. But what he failed to say is that all the chocolates in the box had some kind of sweetness in them. Regardless of our life circumstances, God has a master plan for us. We may not fully be aware of his plan. And sometimes, we will make a turn that does not please him. As I look at Cheryl and I, I see many times God used us for his purposes. Little did we know years ago how our life would turn out or the plans He had for us. Cheryl has touched the lives of so many people. Her faith and positive outlook on life inspires others who are dealing with physical issues. Although she has MS, it doesn't control her. Because of her faith, she has the assurance that she will walk and run again. There are so many family, friends and others that she has touched. She is truly an inspiration of how to approach life when there are obstacles. Cheryl loves and trusts in God. Her attitudes rub off on others. My sons and myself are believers in Jesus Christ because of her testimony. Even with all of her physical issues there is no one I had rather spend my life with. She is the love of my life forever.

As I look back over my life, I cannot ever remember having a Christian man as a role model. Up until I met Cheryl, no one had really spoken to me personally about Jesus. That is really sad, isn't it? Later on, in life, Cheryl's Dad would become a true friend and a role model to me. I could have gone astray. I am so thankful that I placed my faith in Jesus. I ask this question. Men, are you a Christian role model to your children and grandchildren? Men and women, are there younger people that you are pouring your life into? This could be one of the most important things that you will ever do.

Chapter 22

SERVICE TO OTHERS THROUGH THE CHURCH

IN 2016 OUR church went through a major transition. The church approved the idea of being elder led. Not elder ruled, but elder led. (The lead pastor and four laypersons.) If you look into the Scriptures, the early church was fashioned this way. At the same time, our pastor for 23 years was moving to another assignment in his life. The church formed a search committee for another pastor. I was voted to become one of the members of that committee. We were a diverse group of church members. We truly loved the church and wanted it to be successful for God's glory. The Suwanee area is known nationwide as a great place to live. We had many applicants for the job, over 250 resumes. We began the task of working this group down from 250 to 225 to 50 and so on. Each time we cut, one pastor from California was still in the mix.

We narrow the list to five and then to three. He is still one of the ones left in the running. The committee interviews him and his wife. He is the right choice. We realize Suwanee is a diverse and changing community. The church needs a young, new face to carry the church forward. He is called to visit for a weekend and preach. The vote is taken and he is our new pastor. The committee had anticipated losing some of our senior members and we surely did. 150 people left our church. The new Elder board would have their hands full. I was elected to serve on the elder board. The first year was a struggle. There were constant meetings with members who wanted things to stay the same. They wanted things done like it had been for 50 years. It seems like every week, friends that we had known for 20 to 25 years were leaving the church. At the same time, the church's finances were suffering.

Through a lot of prayer, love, endurance, and staying the course, the church on the hill has turned the corner. We start seeing new faces each Sunday. We are beginning to grow in amazing ways. Some ask, "Why are you still at the church?" My answer, "I don't believe God has called me to leave." The future of the church is in the hands of our young believers. But, God can use a senior adult at the church.

So, each week the church gathers to worship and then we go into the community to tell others about Jesus.

Some life lessons from those years: God answers prayer. Love all, even when some are hard to love. Look to God's word for your answers. Trust and know that God is in control of all things. Serve others and give God all the honor and glory for everything you do.

Chapter 23

SALVATION STORIES

I HAD MENTIONED earlier about my older brothers (Jimmy and Leamon) and how I saw them come to know Jesus. Leamon was a fine man, a good father and husband. He was honest, trustworthy and kind. He believed there was a God that created the heavens and earth. But he lacked a true relationship and faith in Jesus as Lord and Savior of his life. Little did I know that God was going to use me as His messenger. In the last few months of Leamon's life, I would go by to see him every few days. I always carried a Bible in my truck. Romans road to salvation was highlighted in it. When I would visit Leamon, I would say that today I would talk to him about his faith. And I would visit and leave without a word. The next visit I would say today is the day and I would come and go without a word. What in the world is wrong with me? This is my brother that needs to know about Jesus. Finally, I visit Leamon and leave my Bible with him. I tell him to look at the Scripture in Romans that I have highlighted.

I will visit again in a few days and we will talk. A few days later I visit and asked if he has read the Scripture that I had highlighted. I also asked him if he has that relationship with Jesus. I explained Jesus came to earth and lived a sinless life, died on the cross for our sins, but death could not hold Him. He arose on the third day and conquered death. He is at the right hand of the Father in Heaven. He is preparing a place for us as believers. Leamon, do you know by faith in Jesus that He has died for your sins and He will once and for all forgive you and restore you to a relationship with a Holy God? Would you like for me to ask our pastor to come by and see you? His reply was "No, I want Jesus in my life today." As fragile as he was, we get on our knees and he asked Jesus to forgive him and to come into his life. Cancer will take him away later but I have the assurance that he is in Heaven and I will see him again.

For many years I thought Jimmy was a believer. He's in the hospital and there's not a lot of hope that he will survive. By accident, I visit him when the Associate Pastor of the church he attends is in the room. As the Pastor leaves, I walk out into the hallway with him. He tells me that each time he and Jimmy visit, he asks Jimmy about his salvation and his relationship with Jesus. Jimmy's reply is "I'm getting closer to doing something about that". This is shocking news to me. A few days later, I visit Jimmy early in the morning. I say to him,

"Jimmy, I love you so much. I want to spend eternity with you in Heaven. Do you know Jesus can give you life forever? All you need to do is ask Him to forgive you and come into your life." In the stillness of the early morning as we hold hands, Jimmy closes his eyes and prays to Jesus, our Lord and Savior. Because of what Jesus did on the cross, Jimmy, by faith in Him has become a child of God.

It is amazing how God can take any one of us and He can use us for His purposes. We can be His messengers to family, friends and strangers. He calls us to share the gospel in our daily walk. It is not about us; it is all about Him. To God be the glory.

REFLECTIONS

As we get closer and closer to the end of this writing, I find myself reflecting back on my life. I had suppressed many things in my life, even to the point that Cheryl was not aware of them. I found it very difficult at times to even write about my early life. Those early years, up until I met Cheryl, could be a book in itself. I often think about times when I did stupid acts, where I could have been seriously injured or even killed. And yet God had a plan for me and He kept me safe. Years ago, as a young boy, we lived near a sawmill in Wrens, Ga. The mill had a large pile of wood shavings. Sometimes spontaneous combustion would catch the pile on fire. I am speaking of a large pile, maybe 30 feet high. The fire would be smoldering deep inside the mountain of shavings. There would be spots that the fire would burn through to the outside. This would create holes in the piles of red hot ashes. Our parents and also the mill workers told us, time after time, to stay off the pile. If we fell into one of those holes, we could be burned or covered over by hot ashes and shavings. What did we do? We climbed to the top of the pile and slid down time after time. You can call it luck or you can call it God's protection on stupid kids. We always made it home safely.

As a teenager, I would do unwise things with cars such as speeding, reckless driving and, yes, mixing alcohol and cars. There were nights when a group of us would gather in Buford and challenge each other on who could be at the Suwanee Grill the fastest. Stupid is what stupid does. Through it all, somehow, I made it home safely.

All of us can reflect on our past, but we can only control our future. I often asked how would my life have ended up without Cheryl? Where would I be or what kind of person would I be without faith in Jesus as my Lord and Savior? I think the answer would be my life would be hopeless, filled with darkness and despair. This morning in our pastor's message, he asked a profound question. Do you walk with God? As I pondered that question, it led me to the following questions. Do I read and study His word? Do I talk to Him daily in prayer? Do I love, honor, trust and obey Him? Does my strength come from Him? Do I realize that God controls every aspect of my life? Do I love Him and does that love rub off to others? I cannot be the husband and caregiver that I am without His love, grace, mercy and strength. What would be your answer to these questions in your life today?

Is our life just one big coincidence or the luck of the draw? Or does God have a plan to use us for His purposes? I truly believe He controls every aspect of our life. How amazing, millions and millions of people and God knows each and every one of us personally.

As we grow older, I think sometimes we may ask ourselves. "What will be my legacy? Will I leave a legacy for my sons, grandchildren, friends and others? Will my sons be able to say that I walked with God? Will my sons be able to say that I loved their mother unconditionally? Will my friends and family be able to look at my life and see the shadow of Jesus all over it?" I trust and pray that is my legacy.

Chapter 24

MILESTONE ANNIVERSARY CELEBRATIONS

THERE ARE MANY events in our life that are significant and call for celebration. Here are the few that come to my mind: our wedding, the birth of our children, our salvation, turning 40 years old and our anniversaries. On our 25th wedding anniversary, our sons carried us out to dinner at one of our favorite steakhouses. Cheryl's brother, Danny and his wife, Lisa surprised us with a party at their home.

Our 30th wedding anniversary was going to be special. We began thinking about something we had never done. We checked into trips to Australia and Europe but the timing and cost were not right. I asked Cheryl, "How would you like to travel down the coast of California right beside the ocean?" Here was our plan. We will leave Atlanta on Thanksgiving Day and fly to San Francisco. I made the reservations at the Marriott Hotel near Fisherman's Wharf for two nights. We rent a car at the airport and drive over to the hotel. During the next two days, we see all that San Francisco has to offer. We saw the wharf area and all the local seafood, the Golden Gate Bridge, Alcatraz, Chinatown and of course the streetcars. They were all part of our visit. What a great time for the two of us.

After two days, we leave and head south on US Highway One. We have no agenda and no reservations for the next two days. We are amazed at the beach and the ocean. On the East Coast, we think of the ocean with long flat beaches.

Here on the West Coast there are places with high cliffs and small beach areas. Some of these areas are breathtaking and so beautiful. We stop every so often just to take in the beauty of God's creation. Before we realize it, the day has passed and it is late afternoon. We're nearing the beach town of Santa Barbara, California. There are a lot of people in this area. Seems like there's some type of festival going on. I begin to stop and check on hotels for the night. After three or four stops, we have found nothing available, all are full. Finally, I see this very nice, fancy hotel right on the beach. I will check to see if there's a room available and if we can afford it. As I entered the lobby, there's a man giving the young lady behind the desk a hard time. He tells her that he has always stayed here and has never had a problem getting a reservation. The young lady behind the counter is very courteous but the man is very rude. Finally, he storms out saying "I'll never stay here again."

I approached the young lady and said "I don't suppose you have another room available for the night. My wife and I are from Georgia and on our 30th anniversary trip." She looks down at the desk and up at me and smiles. "I have only one and it is the Grand Suite. We normally charge $450 per night. But since it is after 5 PM I can reduce it to $200 for the night." I said "I'll take the room" and we check in.

Cheryl and I go up to the second floor and open the door to the room. We are shocked. We have stayed in a lot of very nice hotel rooms and even suites. This one tops the cake. Two sides of the living room are glass windows from top to bottom looking out over the ocean. The bedroom and bathroom are huge. A circular bed is in the center of the room, Jacuzzi tub and glass shower in the bath. It is amazing. We have an early dinner and go back to the room to watch the sunset from the balcony. What a wonderful day we have had.

Early the next morning, we are headed to Los Angeles. It doesn't take us long to see Hollywood and Rodeo Drive. Somehow, we get sidetracked. We stopped for gas and feel very uncomfortable. The gas station attendant is in a bulletproof stall. I believe we are in a section of town that is not on the vacation guide. It is off again and headed south into the farm country of California.

Our next stop is San Juan Capistrano. This is the site of the mission where the birds return each year after their migration. It is a beautiful little Spanish town. Two things I remember about this stop. Cheryl and I had a fantastic Mexican lunch at an outside café. Later that day, we would see a large truck turnover in the middle of town. The trucks whole load of strawberries was spilled all over the street.

Next stop was San Diego. This is one of my favorite towns. I was here during my time in the Navy. We have also vacationed here as a family twice. We check into the hotel overlooking the bay. This is a beautiful city with great weather and great food. Old town San Diego has to be a part of your visit if you are ever here. We visit San Diego for two days. Afterwards we go to the airport, turn in the rental car and make the short flight over to Las Vegas. This is our final stop before heading home. What a wonderful time with the love of my life. We will remember the trip for many years.

OUR 40TH WEDDING ANNIVERSARY

Cheryl's brother, Danny and his wife, Lisa, celebrate their anniversary in November also. They are celebrating 30 years of marriage and we are celebrating 40 years. We plan to cruise together to the Caribbean. We will spend five days of rest, fun and relaxation with our dearest friends. Cheryl and I come back home refreshed and renewed. We are ready to do life together again for another 10 years, God willing.

OUR 50TH WEDDING ANNIVERSARY

I don't know where the years have gone. Can I really be 71 years old? Seems like yesterday our sons were teenagers. I'm so thankful. God has truly blessed me in so many ways.

He's given me Cheryl, the boys, grandchildren and my health and most of all my relationship with Him. About a year and a half before our 50th anniversary, Cheryl and I began thinking about how to celebrate this special time. If we stay at home, the boys will plan something special for us. Why not just carry the whole family on a cruise? We could dedicate the cruise and time together to Della, Cheryl's mother. She loved those family cruises of years ago. We want to do this so it will be remembered by everyone years later. I have contacted Carnival Cruise Lines for accessible guests. They do such a great job for Cheryl's requirements. After hours on the phone, we are all booked. Cheryl and I have a large accessible room with a balcony. I also booked seven more rooms with balconies for the family. Over the next year as the time gets closer and closer, we get more and more excited. Our cruise will be between Christmas and New Year's. In fact, we will be on the ship New Year's Eve. We get together for a family meal at Christmas time. Cheryl gives all the children and grandchildren her cruise rules. Some of the rules were: put on your smiley face, get plenty of sun, laugh, dance, have fun, try to attend dinner each night and a few other things. I can't wait to tell you how all of this turned out.

Chapter 25

OUR 50TH ANNIVERSARY FAMILY CRUISE

IT WAS DECEMBER of 2019 when Jamie, a friend of his, Cheryl and I will leave for the cruise. It is so much better for Cheryl to be rested before boarding on Saturday morning. Seems like we always carry too much stuff. At least we can check it before we board. Saturday morning comes and we arrive at the cruise terminal. Everyone has made the trip down safely. All 17 of us will meet at check-in. We are all excited about the next five days. The cruise lines have really improved check-in and in less than 30 minutes we are on board the ship. Cheryl and I have traveled on this ship before and have stayed in the same room we have this time. The room works so well for Cheryl. She can drive her chair into the bathroom with plenty of room to turn around. It has a roll in shower with a fold-down bench. She can even go out on the balcony with her chair. I call ahead and the ship's crew decorates our room with all kinds of anniversary banners. It was a surprise for Cheryl and it really looks nice. This will be our home away from home for the next five days.

Later Saturday afternoon, we meet up on the Lido deck for lunch and group pictures. Lori has gotten all 17 of us anniversary T-shirts. Everyone has their shirt on for our group picture.

We will have no planned agenda for all of us other than hopefully seeing everyone at the evening dinner table. The ship has really taken care of us. We have two large tables, side by side, where we can all enjoy our dinner together. Can you imagine five nights in a row having your complete family together for dinner? Every single night we had everyone show up. In most cases, the grandchildren were early arrivals. They always dress up and look so nice. This was quality time and the highlight of our day.

I don't know what it is about our room or this ship. But Cheryl and I rest and sleep so well. We would stay up late at night but we would sleep late in the morning. Most mornings I wake and go up on deck for coffee. Cheryl would sleep to 9 or 9:30 each morning and then we would have breakfast together. When our children were off the ship at the beach, Cheryl and I would find a nice quiet place out on the open deck. She would recline in her chair and read. I did of lot of this writing on the ship. We were truly enjoying this relaxing time together.

On the third night there was a show called "The Marriage Test". The cruise director would let the audience choose two couples and one couple would be the longest married couple. Surprisingly, Cheryl and I were the longest married couple in the audience. Each couple was placed back to back. We were asked some funny questions about marriage. The object was to agree on the answers. (Example: the word sex was changed to ice cream). The cruise director would ask, "How many times have had you had ice cream on the ship?"

Cheryl was having a little trouble writing the answers on her clipboard. Lyza, our youngest granddaughter, came up and sat next to Cheryl and wrote her answers for her. Some of the questions were funny, for example: rate your first kiss, where did you have the best ice cream? what is the one thing your spouse does that annoys you? We and the audience had so much fun and laughed and laughed. From then on, anywhere Cheryl and I went on the ship, someone would recognize us as the longest married couple. We met so many very nice people, both young and old. The world is still full of good, honest and loving souls.

New Year's Eve is dress-up night on the ship and boy did our crew fit the occasion.

I've never seen so many sequences in all my life. After dinner, it is party time up on the Lido deck. The band is playing; folks are dancing, laughing and enjoying each other's company. It's a beautiful, starry night. I believe almost every guest on the ship was up on the Lido deck at midnight. What a new year to remember. With Cheryl, the love of my life, and all my family, I could not have been any happier.

It is the final night of the cruise. We've had so much fun being with our family. Our last dinner in the dining room was excellent. They saved the best for last. After dinner we will buy some T-shirts, look at all the pictures the crew has taken and play a bit in the casino. Before we know, it's midnight. It is off to the room for a bath and bedtime. We will have to rise very early in the morning. As I lay in the bed with my arms around the love of my life, I'm looking out the window at the vastness of the oceans, the beauty of the stars and the moon and the sky. I realize how large and mighty our Lord is, the Creator of the heavens and earth and all that we have.

I also realize how small and minute each one of us are. Yet God knows us and knows every detail about our life. I don't know the outcome of Cheryl's life or my life. I do know that God is in charge. And I will hold Cheryl in my arms until God takes us home. Tomorrow is another day. We will go home refreshed and renewed. God willing we are ready to do life together for hopefully another 30 years.

Chapter 26

CORONAVIRUS PANDEMIC

AFTER ARRIVING HOME from our cruise, we keep seeing the news about a new virus in China. There are thousands of people infected and some are dying. We think, this is thousands of miles away, how can it ever affect us? Then the news comes that there are cases of the virus in Europe. It is spreading very rapidly. It is also spreading to the United States. It appears that about 1% of those infected are dying. Most of these people are 65 years old or older and have a pre-existing condition. This is a very serious situation for America.

Our economy is beginning to suffer also. The stock market is dropping sharply each day. Businesses are closing or shortening their hours of operation. Restaurants are going to take out service only. There are no bars or nightclubs open. Our government is telling us to keep our distance from each other and, if possible, to shelter in. In fact, in some states this is mandatory.

I can never recall seeing anything quite like this. People are almost on the verge of panic. They are buying everything they can in the stores. The shelves are almost empty of all hand sanitizers, Lysol sprays and wipes and, for some reason, paper towels and toilet paper. One week or so ago, if you were to go to one of the big box stores, people would be buying carloads of paper products. I would not have a place to store that many rolls of paper. And now there is no toilet paper to be found. When the stores do receive a shipment, there will be a limit of one package per customer. That's a real good thing.

Churches are cancelling their gatherings and doing online messaging. Our church has done two Sundays online. In late March, there is no timetable for any corporate gatherings to resume. I am thankful we have the technical ability for our pastor to stand in his living room and proclaim the gospel to our church.

Cheryl has pretty much sheltered in for the last two weeks. The pool complex is closed. She is truly missing her weekly water exercises. Angie is doubling up on her exercises at home. Hopefully this will not last much longer.

How has this affected Cheryl and me? Well, we sure have spent some quality time together. She and I both have done a lot of reading and studying. I also have spent many hours writing and working on the book. We really miss going out for dinner. I had first thought that I would end the book the last day of the cruise. But when all of this surfaced, I believed it was important to put on paper my thoughts, feelings and how we approach this bump in the road of life.

You might ask us if we are concerned about the virus? The answer is yes. We're doing everything in our power to avoid it. Washing our hands, cleaning and disinfecting surfaces and avoiding contact with others has become a part of our daily routine. Are we worried or even fearful? The answer is no. God is sovereign and He is in control. By our faith in Jesus Christ, we have the assurance of life eternal without sickness or disease. As we did in the past in our lives, we are to stay the course and trust in God. He will never leave nor forsake us. This is His promise.

March 31 2020

It is the end of March and the coronavirus is still with us. In fact, it is increasing in infections and deaths. The latest deaths worldwide are 32,000 people. In the United States 2800 people have lost their life. Just in a 24-hour period, there have been over 300 deaths in the United States. The President and his team last night increased the social distancing until the end of April. For us over 65 years old that means staying at home if possible. The doctors on the government's coronavirus team say there could be as many as 100,000 deaths nationwide before this is all over. That is a lot of folks. By comparison 38,000 to 40,000 lives are lost each year in car accidents in the United States. In all the years of the war in Vietnam, 58,000 US soldiers would lose their life. This virus is going to take a tragic toll on our country.

We pray for the families of those affected by this deadly virus. We also pray for all the medical personnel, those who are battling this disease daily. Father, we pray that you rid our country of this pandemic.

Cheryl and I are doing well. She has only been out of the house one time in two weeks. One of the biggest things she misses is not going to the pool. Water exercising has been really good for her. We also miss our church family. We are thankful for the online messages, but the corporate gathering has always been a part of our life. This Easter Sunday will probably be a little different for us. But regardless of where we will be on Easter, we will still celebrate that Jesus Christ conquered death and arose from the grave. Our hope is in Him and only Him. It sounds as though the next few weeks, even months, are going to be a challenge for all of us. So, what do we do? We should do everything possible to slow the spread of the virus. We can have quality family time. We can get some of those things done around the house that we've been putting off. We can check on our friends, neighbors and family, especially the senior members. Most of all, we can pray and pray again. I would also suggest that you look into God's word. Many times in the Scriptures God's people were faced with terrible situations. But he loved them, cared for them and never did forsake them. He does the same thing for us today. Trust in God; He is in control.

APRIL 4 2020

Cheryl and I are staying at home almost all the time. I go out for food and medicine when needed. We continue to wash our hands. Lysol spray and wipes are used in our home quite often. We miss the contact with our family and friends. We have not hugged any of our grandchildren in weeks. Our weekly routine of going to dinner with our sons or Cheryl's brother and his wife has completely stopped. We are people persons. There is a big empty space in our lives.

Here are some of the facts on the situation as of today. The governor of Georgia issued a stay at home order on April 1 to expire at the end of the month. He also closed all the schools for the remainder of the year. The joys of seeing our granddaughters playing sports disappeared until next year. In Georgia, as of today, there are 4000 confirmed cases with 154 deaths. Our County (Hall) has 71 confirmed cases as of today. These are tough times for our country. Some of the experts on the virus tell us we are not at the highest peak of the infection. The worst is yet to come.

So, how are we living with peace within our heart during this time of coronavirus?

1) We're making a habit of washing our hands quite often.

2) We are bathing our hearts in God's truth. We believe that Jesus Christ is Lord and Savior of our life.

3) We are looking into the Bible for His promises of comfort and care.

   A) Colossians 3:15: "Let the peace of Christ rule in your hearts, since as members of one body you were called to peace. And be thankful". Colossians 3:16: "Let the message of Christ dwell among you richly as you teach and admonish one another with all wisdom through Psalms, hymns, and songs from the spirit, singing to God with gratitude in your hearts."

   B) Psalm 23:4 " Even though I walk through the valley of the shadow of death, I will fear no evil. For you are with me, your rod and your staff, they comfort me."

C) Psalm 9:9 "The Lord is a stronghold for the oppressed, a stronghold in times of trouble."

4) We are to stop worrying and continue to pray, thanking God for all His blessings. We don't know what the future holds for us. But God does. He will hear our prayers and forgive us of our sins and yes; he will heal our land.

A) Philippians 4:6 "Do not be anxious about anything, but in everything by prayer and supplication with thanksgiving let your requests be made known to God."

April 10, 2020 Good Friday

Today is a special day in the life of Christians. Good Friday is a day of mourning and sorrow over the sacrificial death of Jesus Christ. Yet, it is also a day of gratitude for the supreme sacrifice that Jesus made for us. Darkness came on this day but hope is coming. A glorious light will shine on Easter Sunday morning. We will celebrate a risen Savior.

This has been a tragic week in the life of our nation. There are a total of 16,700 deaths nationwide as of Friday from the virus. Georgia has had a total of 412 deaths so far from the virus.

This morning I saw a cartoon with Snoopy standing against a wall drinking a cup of coffee. His question was, "What do I do about this coronavirus?" And underneath the picture was his reply, "Wash your hands often, drink your coffee, listen to some worship music and let God handle the rest." We should be concerned but we also should know that God is in control.

This will be a very different Easter Sunday for Cheryl and me. There will not be a typical sunrise service or a gathering of our church family. But we will awake and celebrate a risen Savior who gave His life for us. Death could not have power over Him. He is alive and well. He is our Lord and Savior. When we are faced with situations beyond our control, we can call on His power and strength in the darkest of days. So, what will Cheryl and I do on Easter Sunday morning? We will listen to the online message. We will pray for those families affected by the virus. We will thank God that we have each other. But most of all we will thank God for Jesus, our Lord and Savior.

Isaiah 41:10 "Fear not for I am with you; be not dismayed, for I am your God; I will strengthen you, I will help you, I will uphold you with My righteous right hand." (ESV)

So as Cheryl and I approach the coming weeks, how are we coping with the anxiety of the coronavirus? I guess, as in all other unknowns, it is normal to feel anxious about the pandemic. We're truly thankful that we have no signs or symptoms of the virus. We only know of one family member, a cousin's daughter-in-law, who has been infected so far. So how are we spending our days together? We are trying to limit our exposure to the news media. We spend a lot of time reading and studying and check the news only once or twice each day. Sometimes I will type in a Bible question and spend hours exploring some of my trusted commentaries. Also, I look for new recipes that I can cook. I found a recipe the other day for stuffed shells. They were really good. We try to keep fruits, vegetables and nuts around to snack on. It is so easy to overeat when you're at home 24 -7.

Cheryl spends a lot of time on the phone checking on family and friends. Yesterday, she was on the phone for over an hour with one of her best friends.

I believe one thing that helps us, is to focus on the things that we are grateful for. While things are challenging and uncertain, they are also good things in our daily lives. In your spare time I would recommend making a daily list of all the things you're grateful for. You will be surprised at how many you come up with. This is also a perfect time to develop the habit of a scheduled quiet time with our Lord. He will give you strength and peace.

Psalm 29:11 "The Lord will give strength to His people; The Lord will bless His people with peace." (ESV)

April 24, 2020

The President and his task force have released a plan for opening up the country. There are millions of people out of work. We have got to get the country moving again. Many people received the stimulus check this week. But for those not working this money will not last long.

I went to Athens, Georgia on Thursday with my son. He has a job site in downtown Athens. The town looks like a ghost town. With it being a college town, there are no students in town. Most all the restaurants, bars, nightclubs, coffee shops, barbershops and everything else are closed. I'm really concerned that some of those businesses will not be able to resume business after this is all over. This is true throughout the country.

Cheryl and I are doing quite well. I'm concerned about her not getting enough exercise. Hopefully the pool will open real soon. She is also struggling with a UTI infection. She is on antibiotics that normally help after about three days. I told her the other day that when this is all over, we're going to eat out every night for two weeks. I have run out of things to cook.

As of Friday, there have been over 33,000 deaths from the virus in the United States. This is a tragedy. We pray for all the families affected by the silent killer. According to all the professional sources, we are very close to the crest of the hill. We should begin to see a downturn in infections and deaths. As a nation, God willing, we will return to normal life soon. As difficult as it may seem we must keep our eyes focused on God and thank him for his mercy and grace in our daily lives.

April 30, 2020

We're still sheltering in place (staying at home). We have heard the words: data, charts, infection, ventilators, I C U and recorded deaths for almost 6 weeks. Cheryl and I are so ready for all of this to be behind us.

Here are the latest numbers. As of April 28, the United States has 56,500 deaths. Georgia has 1025 deaths and Hall County 15 deaths.

All the experts on the virus tell us we are on the downhill side of the curve. In fact, the governor of Georgia on April 24 opened some non-essential businesses. Barbershops, hair salons, gyms, tattoo parlors and other business were allowed to open with many guidelines. Some restaurants were allowed to open on Monday, April 27 for inside seating. This decision by the governor of Georgia was met with both approval and opposition. I'm sure the news media will be watching the charts on Georgia for the next few weeks. I surely hope our governor is a hero and not a zero.

This is where Cheryl and I are at now. I'm thankful that we are not only husband and wife, but we are the best of friends. This is really helpful while we are spending so much time together. Both of us have to work really hard on showing patience and kindness. I admit we fail at times. These are difficult times. I pray that our relationship with God and with each other matures and grows stronger each day. My concern right now is for Cheryl, she is getting so stiff. Even though Angie and I exercise her daily, she misses three days a week at the pool. Please, I pray that it opens soon. Last night as I was getting her in the tub. She slipped and almost fell. I was able to get her back in her power chair with great difficulty. She had hit her leg on the corner of the tub and cut her shin. After a Band-Aid and repositioning her, we started all over again and got her in the tub safely. I'm so thankful that God gives me the strength and ability to move Cheryl around daily.

Over the last few weeks, Cheryl and I have spent many hours on the book. She has begun to correct grammar and punctuation. I cannot believe all the mistakes I have made. Cheryl is such a big help in this area. I don't thank her enough. Hopefully, over the next few weeks, I can come to a conclusion with the book and move on to some professional editing.

These past few weeks have been one of the most unusual times in our life. Cheryl and I have never experienced anything quite like this. As we sit here this afternoon we began to think. What are we truly missing during this time?

1) Our family (hugs from our grandchildren)

2) Our church family

3) Dinner with friends and family

4) Short day or weekend trips

5) Social gathering with friends

6) Sports-high school, college, professional

7) Shopping and swimming for Cheryl

But there are many things we are thankful and grateful for. Here's a list of just a few of those.

1) The love we share for each other.

2) We are thankful for our health.

3) Jesus is real to both of us.

4) God is in control and sovereign over everything.

5) We are not hurting financially.

6) We have food, clothing and shelter.

7) We live in the greatest country on earth.

8) We have freedom to express our opinions.

9) This virus and hard times are only temporary.

10) We are thankful we still have our 12-year-old bulldog, Sampson.

Let us all remember; God knows all things. They are better days to come. This difficult time will be behind us. Stay Faithful.

Chapter 27

LIFE GOES ON

AS I COME to the close of the book in May 2020, the coronavirus is still present. But it does appear that the infections and deaths are slowly going down. Hopefully, we are past the worst part of this awful virus. Maybe we can return to some form of normal life. For most of us, this has been an once-in-a-lifetime experience. Throughout the whole ordeal, we can rely on this truth: God has been with us and He is present every day of our life.

I pose these questions as I reflect on this time of Corona virus:

1) Will I be better or will I be bitter after this experience?

2) Has this time at home been put to good use?

3) Have I done things that helped my neighbors and friends?

4) Have I remained close to God through prayer and study?

5) Have I found my purpose in life?

6) Is God guiding me to do something in life that I have been putting off?

7) Do I have a dream that I have not fulfilled?

8) Do I know my gifts that God has given me?

I would pray that you could find a quiet time to reflect upon these questions. We are never too old to start something that will honor our God.

So, as I come to the end of our story, I hope and pray that something you have read will influence how you go about living your daily life with others. I fully understand that all marriages will not work. All we can do as believers in Christ is to apply his principles to our marriage and pray that our spouse does the same. We cannot control the hearts and minds of others. Things that were said in the book applied to our marriage. They don't necessarily apply to all marriages. Please understand I am not special; I am not different. I came into the world as a poor, southern, country boy. God had a plan for my life, just as he does for yours. It was 19 years before I realized that I could not live without Him. I needed Jesus every day of my life. I cannot fix every obstacle that I face. But because of my faith in Jesus, He is always with me and controls every aspect of my life.

We must always remember that our relationship and love of our spouse, children and others is so important. It can only be obtained when we have a relationship with a Holy God. We need to fully realize the love He showed for us by dying on the cross for our sins. He is full of mercy and grace. He tells us to love Him and love our neighbor. I asked you a question. Can you truly say that you love your spouse uncon-ditionally? Always, in any marriage there will be times of sickness and health, times of financial security and insecurity and times of joy and sadness. This is all part of this life here on earth. Don't let those bumps in the road of life become hills that are impossible for you to climb. Trust in God, He is always with us. Finally, we must love our spouse with all our heart and our entire mind and all our soul till death do us part.

As we proceed with the task of editing and publishing this book. There could be some side notes added at the end of this writing. These notes would pertain to the coronavirus and how Cheryl and I coped with getting back to some form of normal life.

I hope and pray that this writing will be beneficial to you along life's road. May God bless you and your family in the coming days?

Here it is April 2020. So much as happened in our life and the life of our nation. I felt it important to add these things at the end of the book. Some of these events will be things our children and grandchildren will discuss and study many years after we've gone to be with Jesus.

CHERYL AND MS

I had mentioned earlier that because of the virus in the closing of the aquatic center, Cheryl was getting very little exercise. This has taken a toll on her physically. She is not moving as well as before the virus. On a couple of occasions, I almost let her fall as she was getting into the tub. In fact, we have begun using the lift equipment the last few months. It's a simple process, but it does take a little more time. I place a nylon seat in her power chair. The overhead winch is attached to the seat. It lifts her up and transfers her over and into the tub. This is just another step we are adding to our daily routine. Cheryl remains very positive and she is full of the words "thank you." From my perspective, I find myself at times becoming very frustrated. I have to be so careful with my tone of voice and my attitude. I will admit that at times I lose it. I've always got to remember how much we love each other. We are in God's hands and He knows the outcome of our lives.

Those old questions pop up in my mind occasionally. Why me? Why Cheryl? Could it be better somewhere else? Is the grass greener on the other side of the fence? I heard a preacher say the other day, "Yes, the grass is greener on the other side. But there could be a septic tank hidden underneath that pretty, green grass".

So, where are my emotions daily? I have to find that place and time to reflect and pray. I cannot do this alone. My strength is not enough. I'll rely on a holy God that can do all things. I tell myself daily, hold on, hold on, be the man, be the husband that God looks down on and smiles saying "my good and faithful servant". So, we will take life one day at a time. We will thank God daily for the time He gives us together until He takes us home.

THE VIRUS

The Coronavirus is still with us. The death total is around 200,000 people in the United States. Cheryl and I have begun to go places including church. But we practice distancing and wear our facemask. It is almost comical. We go out to eat and some people will only remove their mask long enough to eat.

I saw a man and a woman driving down the road the other day, Windows up, and both had facemasks on. I suppose the virus had infiltrated the inside of the car.

Our government officials are saying we may have a vaccine near the end of the year. That will be a blessing to many people.

Early in the book, I spoke of my friend during high school. We were informed a few weeks ago that he had passed from the virus after two weeks in the hospital and about one week on the ventilator. It was so sad; we could not visit Allen in his final days of his life. Other friends and acquaintances have weathered the virus and are doing quite well afterwards. We also learned on Friday, October 2 that Pres. Trump and his wife have tested positive for the virus. He has been admitted to Walter Reed hospital so the doctors can monitor his condition more closely. We pray for his full recovery.

In Our Nation

To be perfectly honest, we are in a mess. Throughout the last few months, there has been civil unrest in many of our cities. A very small percentage of law enforcement officers have made some very unwise and unjust decisions. To sum it up, we as a nation under God cannot condone the loss of one innocent life or the destruction of others property. I pray daily that our nation can come together as brothers and sisters. We can agree to disagree and still be joined by the unity of one nation under God. The election of the president of the United States is only 40 days away. There is much division between both parties on how the country should be governed.

Another thing of importance in our government, recently one of our Supreme Court justices passed away. The president is in the process of appointing her replacement. There will be many hours of questioning, discussion, and voting in the Senate before she is confirmed. This is a lifetime appointment and can change the look of the court for many years.

With all of this going on, where is our hope? What do we hold fast to? God is in charge. He is sovereign over all things. Yes, He knows how long the coronavirus will last. He knows how many lives will be lost. He's in charge. We need to remember that Jesus is our King. He has promised us that He will always be with us regardless of who sits in the White House. Our prayer will always be that our nation will have an awakening; that we will be one nation under God. "In God We Trust" will be stamped on all of our hearts and minds.

CLOSER TO HOME SAMPSON, OUR BELOVED ENGLISH BULLDOG

I never believed that Cheryl and I could become so attached to an animal. Our son, Andy, got Sam when he was six weeks old. We adopted him when he was three years old. In April 2020 Sam turned 12 years old. That is a long life for bulldog. Sam would leave us on July 6, 2020. I will try to place on paper some of the emotions I felt during his final days with us

JULY 3, 2020

Sampson is not doing well. He can hardly walk. I have to pick him up and carry him outside to do his business. Sometimes, if I touch him on his hip, he will bark or even snap at me. He is also doing something very strange. Sam has always been a people dog. He likes to be right under Cheryl or I. The past few days, we will find him in the office under the desk or hiding in a corner of the house. That is not like our buddy. The decision is made; we will carry him to the Vet on Monday and say our goodbyes. How we would love to keep him longer, just a few months. That would be very selfish on our part. The time has come. Sadly, Monday is coming far too soon.

It has been a tradition over the past few years on Saturday mornings; Sam and I would share bacon, egg biscuit together. I go down to the local sandwich shop and pick up our breakfast. When I return, Sam hobbles into the kitchen from the bedroom. This will be our final breakfast together. Monday is coming.

JULY 6, 2020

I called the vet's office and arranged to have Sam at his office by 9:30 AM. Sam has always loved to ride and today is no different. When I say to him, Sam "let's go for a ride" his ears stood up and he tried to walk to the door. I pick him up and put him on the passenger seat for his final ride. I physically carry him into the vet's office. They place us in a room and the nurse prepares Sampson for the injection. The vet comes in and tells me I can spend all the time I need with Sampson. They place a nice blanket on the floor and he and I love on each other for a time. The moment has come, the vet gives Sampson the injection and a minute later he breathed his last breath. This hurts in ways that I've never imagined. It was the final chapter in the life of our four-legged friend. We will have Sam cremated and spread his ashes later on.

Throughout the years, I've been with a lot of Christian people when they passed and went to Heaven. But this was totally different with Sam. I had never experienced these emotions before. There's an empty place in our home tonight and for many days afterwards. Cheryl will shed tears many times for many days. I know dogs don't have souls. But I believe, because Sam gave Cheryl and I so much joy, we will see him in heaven. Sampson, we will always love you and cherish your memories.

These words are not to discourage anyone from having four-legged friends. The joys they give you far outweigh the pain of seeing them pass. After a while, Cheryl and I will have another friend to share our home with.

ANGIE, OUR DEAR FRIEND AND CAREGIVER TO CHERYL

Angie has been with us for 17 years. She has truly become a part of our family. Cheryl and I love her as if she was our daughter. In July 2020 Angie began looking for a job that would provide retirement and insurance. I cannot provide these things for her although I would surely like to. She has found a position as a nurse at a local high school. Angie informs us that August 1 will be her last day. Angie's college-age daughter, Autumn, will step into her role until December 31, 2020. We knew that the time would come when Angie would leave us. Both of us are very sad, yet happy, for her. She's been a blessing over the years. She did so many small things for us. But most important, she really looked after Cheryl. I always knew when Cheryl was with Angie that she was being taken care of.

I had mentioned early in the book that there are bumps and hills on this road of life. Some are just unavoidable. This is one that Cheryl and I must deal with. We are actively looking for another caregiver. We have put the word out with our friends and family and also our church. We have some time thanks to Autumn for filling in for us. We are confident that God will provide. We pray that the right person will enter our life in the coming weeks.

In November and December we are interviewing people for the caregiver job.

As, we come to the close of 2020 and the beginning of 2021. There are a few things that will influence our life that I must mention.

CHERYL'S NEW CAREGIVER

God has blessed us with a very sweet lady. She is a sister to one of our church members. Zeni has recently moved from New York City to our area. She is living with her sister and brother-in-law. Zeni has gone through three weeks of on-the-job training. Cheryl and I think she is doing very well and will be a perfect fit for our needs.

JANUARY 5, 2021

On a sad note, Zeni called us and informed us that she had tested positive for the coronavirus. Needless to say, she, as well as Cheryl and I, are in self-imposed quarantine for a few days. Zeni has the typical symptoms but is beginning to feel better. We don't know the outcome of the situation. It is just another bump in the road of life. But without a doubt, God is in complete control.

OUR NEW FOUR-LEGGED FRIEND

Our beloved Sampson will never be forgotten. Cheryl and I think of him quite often. He gave us so much joy.

Our new friends' name is Susie. She is a 12-week-old Shih Tzu. Susie is a ball of energy. She loves to play and wants to be next to Cheryl and I all the time. We have some work to do with her though; She loves to bite on everything, including toes. Hopefully, she will grow out of this stage of her life.

Susie is amazing at night. We place her in her small cage around 10:30 PM and she will sleep all night long. I get her out around 5:30 AM and take her outside. She's added some daily duties to our life, but she will be a joy in our life hopefully for many years. She can disappear in a second. We were in panic mode on two occasions. We lost her in the house for a few minutes and were thinking that she had possibly gotten outside. After friends, neighbors and family looked inside and outside, finally our granddaughter found her scared to death underneath the corner of our bed. So, we are a little more careful with her location these days.

Would you consider it unusual for a 72-year-old man and a 12-week-old puppy to have a conversation? The other afternoon, while Cheryl was gone to the pool. I took Susie in my arms and told her all about Sampson. I told her how much we loved him and how much he loved us. For 9 ½ years, Sampson was a part of our family. We fed him, bathed him and provided him a warm place in the winter and cool place in the summer. Susie, that rug that you pull on in front of the fireplace is where your brother, Sampson, used to lay and sleep many hours each day. He was a big boy. Sampson weighed around 60 pounds. Susie, that's 12 times more than you weigh. Susie, I know you and Sampson would've been the best of friends. Sampson is still with us in our hearts and yes; we have him in a box in the laundry. Susie, you will never replace Sampson. He gave us so much joy. But I know over the course of time you will also bring us all sorts of joy. I promise you, we will be good to you. We will feed you and keep you clean and provide a loving home for you to live in. If Sampson is where I think he is, he's looking down on our home and smiling for you and for Cheryl and I.

OUR NATION AND THE VIRUS

We have seen the election of a new president. It was a very close race with many emotions very high on both sides. Cheryl and I, although we didn't vote for the new president, we will support him because of our love for our country. We need to always remember that God is in control regardless of who sits in the White House.

JANUARY 5, 2021

This was a sad day in the life of our nation. Protesters, rioters, infiltrated the Capital Building while Congress was in session. Damage was done to the building, inside and out. But more important, there was a loss of life may be as many as five souls. As a Christian and a citizen of the United States, I am truly heart-broken. We've got to come together as a nation. We should be able to disagree in a peaceful and non-violent way. I believe God is looking down on us with sadness. I pray for changed hearts and a drawing nearer to God.

FACTS ABOUT THE CORONAVIRUS

The numbers are astonishing and have touched the lives of so many people. As of January 7, there have been 21.7 million confirmed cases in the United States. The loss of life is at 367,662. In a 24-hour period on January 7, they were 4,000 reported deaths in the United States. This virus is like nothing ever experienced in my lifetime. As Cheryl and I sit in self-imposed quarantine, the situation has become very real in our lives.

I came across something from my go to person, Charles Spurgeon, the other day. I quote "I wish, my brothers and sisters, that during this year you may live nearer to Christ than you ever have before. Depend upon it, is when we think much of Christ's that we think little of ourselves, little of our troubles, and little of the doubts and fears that surround us." So how should Cheryl and I look at the situation? We should do all that we can to prevent infection, isolation to some degree, wear our mask in public places and maintain 6 feet social distancing from others. But, most of all our focus should be on above and not on our fears.

FINAL EDITION FEBRUARY 26, 2021

I would like to share with you an update on Cheryl's new caregiver-Zeni. She has been a blessing in our lives. She is doing so well with Cheryl. Zeni seems to be able to transfer and move Cheryl around as well as I can. She has a great attitude and is always smiling. I believe Zeni and Cheryl are becoming really good friends. This makes my life so much easier when I know that Cheryl is taken care of when I'm not present. It seems that over the past few months, Cheryl is having more trouble with her legs. Sometimes her knees will give way and whoever is moving her must be ready to catch her. This is just another obstacle that we will face and overcome. I thank God every day that he gives me the strength and the endurance to look after my beloved wife.

THE CORONAVIRUS

Cheryl and I made it through the self-imposed quarantine in January. We have really been blessed. Who would have ever believed that we would be asked to not attend church or other gatherings; that we would be asked to not have family get-togethers; that it would be wise for us to wear a face covering and social distance in public? This has been a year like no other in our life. Hopefully we are on a downhill slope with the virus. It seems the infections and deaths throughout the United States have decreased. Through the amazing work of doctors, scientists, private companies and government officials we have seen a vaccine developed and distributed throughout the United States. At this time the vaccine is being given to caregivers, first time responders, those in the medical field and persons over 65 years old. It is a two-dose vaccine.

Cheryl and I received our first dose three weeks ago and this past Monday we received our final dose. We had very little complications other than a little bit of soreness in our arm. Doctors tell us that after 14 days from the second shot we will be 95% to 96% protected. Hopefully, and prayerfully, over the course of the next few months we can get back to some type of normal life. I pray for those families that have lost loved ones to the virus. I also thank God daily that he protected our family.

As I come to the close of this writing, it has been a journey like no other. It has challenged me, it has drawn me closer to my God and it has made me appreciate all those simple things of life. But most of all, it has made me realize how important it is to have faith in Jesus. He promises us a life free from sickness and tears; a life in the presence of a Holy God that will last for eternity. Do you know him? Do you know Jesus as your best friend? If not, I pray that today would be the day that you would place your faith in him. He is our answer when all else fails.

Chapter 28

CONCLUSION & CHERYL'S STORY

Conclusion

THERE IS NEVER a good time to end a story, especially when the story is not complete. But there comes a time and a place to close out this writing and the time is now. The last year has been a very unusual year in our life. We don't know what the future holds for Cheryl and I. We do hold firm that a loving God looks down on us and cares and protects us. After 51 years of marriage, we're still in love with each other. Yes, physically we've changed. Our bodies are not as firm as they were. We don't hear or see as well as we did years ago. Our hair is graying, and our skin is thinner and wrinkled. But we are blessed, Cheryl and I have a loving family and we have each other.

Final words: Hold fast to our loving God (Jesus Christ), holdfast to each other (man and wife), stay the course, never give up, because yes everything is going to be just fine.

John 6:47 Truly, truly, I say to you, whoever believes has eternal life. (ESV)

CHERYL'S STORY

I am the one that is blessed to be Donnie Thigpen's wife. I was almost 16 years old when Donnie moved to Suwanee. I didn't have any classes with him but Suwanee was so small that everybody there knew when a new person came to town. I knew his father had just passed away and that Donnie and his mother, younger brother and sister moved to town to be close to his older brother. I didn't have much contact with Donnie but I did notice that he was strong and good-looking. He was a hunk! (In the 60s it was flattering to be called a hunk.)

I didn't really think any more about Donnie until we were seniors in high school. We rode the same bus to school (believe it or not, everybody didn't have a car back then). Donnie seemed very mature to me. He was working 40 hours a week on a night shift. I was excited when he asked me out. We went to the drive-in movie and saw "Thunder Road".

I was glad when he asked me out again. I had dated other people before but was never serious about anyone. I wasn't allowed to date every night but I was allowed to go to church anytime. Donnie became a regular at our church. He had never made a decision to accept Christ as his Savior. In May before we graduated from high school on the Friday night of a weeklong revival, Donnie came forward and made that decision. I was so thrilled! I knew then that he was the man that I wanted to marry. We were both very young but we both knew we wanted to be together until the day we died. My family liked Donnie and I think his family liked me. We were both in college and the draft and the Vietnam War was going on. We wanted to marry and to be together as much as possible. We had no money or worldly possessions. We lived on love and couldn't be happier! After Donnie graduated, he enlisted in the Navy. Being separated was very hard but I was very proud of my handsome husband. After he finished active duty, we settled down and bought a house. Donnie had matured and grown so much in his spiritual life. We were ready to start a family. God blessed us with three wonderful sons. Donnie was a great husband and father. It was not hard for me to submit to him. My father was the head of our household so it was what I expected from Donnie.

If your husband loves you like Christ loves the church, what could be better? I think the world would be so much better if more men would be Christian leaders of their homes. My sons are strong, honest, hard working and smarter because of their dad's example and leadership.

My goal in life has always been to be a wife and mother of a Christian family. God and Donnie have given me both of those. My family has given me so much happiness. My sons, daughter-in-laws and grandchildren have also given me great joy.

I am so thankful for my godly husband. He has shown me so much love and care through many difficult times. I know some men would have turned- tail and run. Thank you, Donnie, for your love and commitment. Your love and devotion to God and family is tremendous. Thank you for being such a godly and loving husband. Donnie, you are my hero!

ACKNOWLEDGEMENTS

THIS BOOK WOULD not have been possible without the help of two people

First, my dear wife, Cheryl, encouraged me throughout this long process. I would get so frustrated that I would want to quit and her encouragement to stay the course allowed me to complete our story. She spent hours editing and the result is the story of Cheryl and me doing life together when we were faced with many of life's obstacles. I am forever grateful for her love and all she did to make this possible.

Also, Becky DeWitt, my dear friend and Christian sister gave countless hours to this endeavor. Because of her tireless efforts this book became a reality. She is listed as co-author and it is a well-deserved title. Without her knowledge and professional insight, we may never have reached completion of this project. I am forever indebted to Becky and thank her from the bottom of my heart.

CPSIA information can be obtained
at www.ICGtesting.com
Printed in the USA
LVHW071336261021
701597LV00021B/799